Europe of Many Circles

Europe of Many Circles

Constructing a Wider Europe

Richard Body

New European Publications
London

British Library Cataloguing in Publication Data
Body, Richard

Europe of Many Circles: Constructing a Wider Europe.
1. European Community
I. Title
341.2422

1. Destiny or Delusion? (with Douglas Evans and others.) Victor Gollancz
2. Freedom and Stability in the Western World. (with Douglas Evans, E. F. Schumacher and others) Croon Helm
3. Agriculture: The Triumph and the Shame. Maurice Temple Smith
4. Farming in the Clouds. Maurice Temple Smith.
5. Red or Green for Farmers. Broad Leys
6. Our Food: Our Land. Century Hutchinson. To be published shortly.

First published by New European Publications Limited 1990
14-16 Carroun Road, London SW8 1JT

Copyright © 1990 by Sir Richard Body

ISBN 1-872410-01-4

Typeset by Mandeville Press, Leigh-on-Sea, Essex

Printed and bound in Great Britain by Biddles Limited, Guildford, Surrey

John Coleman, the editor of *New European* made many helpful suggestions for this book and thought of its title. Alison Prager and John Rattray were responsible for production and undertook the tedious task of correcting the proofs; and the no less tedious business of typing out the manuscript was done most patiently by Melissa Church. I am much in their debt.

Contents

Introduction

Europe — the continent of some thirty-five countries,
that is — now has the chance to end a thousand years
of history.

Her history has had a single theme: of how her nations
have formed unions and alliances, one against another;
and as each one has been dissolved or, more usually,
destroyed by war, new unions or alliances have taken
their place. Self-evidently, these divisions have pitilessly
set European against European. Part of this history has
been the European Community, a union of the West in
fear of the East. The latter's union now shattered, ought
we not to seek a way to end that long catalogue of self-
destructing divisions that has brought such misery to
Europe?

The European Community seems to be handicapped
on three grounds from being the means to that end. As a
supranational authority, it can only function by taking a
great deal of power away from all its member-states; as a
customs union, it has made itself commercially inward-

looking; and, above all, its membership is exclusive. Do these handicaps render the Community out of date, even obsolescent, as the means to a united Europe? To form any other conclusion is difficult. Yet there is much that the peoples of Europe should do together. Their interests demand it, but seldom will it be desirable for all of them to act and behave as one. There are circles of interest that include some nations and exclude others. These circles overlap; and what is needed is some institutional process to co-ordinate these overlapping circles. Is this a new role for the European Community? Reformed, it could be the means to a new Europe at last at peace with herself.

What are the most important interests that can link the nations of Europe together? Are they industrial and agricultural as they were when the Treaty of Rome brought together the original Six in 1957? Or have conditions changed since then to enable us to think of other reasons for the countries of Europe to work together? The answer seems crucial, for will it not decide whether the wounds of Europe's sad divide are allowed to heal or made to fester?

Perhaps the answer came from M. Jean Monnet just before he died. To him more than anyone else we owe the birth of the European Economic Community. When his life was commemorated at a ceremony in Brussels in 1988, M. Chaban Delmas, the former Prime Minister of France, recounted how, shortly before his death, Monnet told a friend that if he were beginning again he would wish the Community to be founded not upon economics but culture. Our cultural values, he might have added, influence our outlook on most things of this world and how we behave in nearly every circumstance. How we treat our environment is undoubtedly decided by our culture. The Amazonian Indians, for example, believe that everything they do and say throughout their lives should be in harmony with nature; and indeed that is the bedrock of their culture. We in Europe are being forced to acknowledge that our own behaviour has fallen far below this ideal and that we are in great danger if we do not change. The concern transcends any frontier, and nowhere in Europe can there be a thinking man or woman oblivious to it.

How we can cope with these concerns in Europe is a major theme of this book. Are they not important enough to end the divisions of Europe? That they belong to Europe was a point forcefully made by the Malaysian Prime Minister at the Commonwealth Conference in October 1989. It is not the countries of the Third World, he said, that are guilty of plundering the planet except when they import the cultural values of the West. Development of the Third World has been held self-evidently desirable, yet we now realise it brings intense pressure upon natural resources, wildlife, soil and everything else pertaining to the environment. No part of the world has travelled for so long on the road of development as Europe. This gives all who live in Europe, whether in the East or the West, a particular responsibility to set an example to the rest cf the world which no individual country can do by itself.

Can Britain stand apart in this? For a century and a half, Britain's geographical semi-detachment from Europe was underscored by the fact that she had more commercial and imperial interests in other continents than in her own. The slaughter of millions in two World Wars, both stemming from treaty obligations, was enough to persuade two generations that it was possible to get too entangled with the affairs of Europe. So powerful arguments could be made to the British people that they would prosper more by keeping their distance. Geography may still allow Britain, if her people so wish, to keep a modest distance from many of the concerns of continental Europe. But environmentally, if for no other reason, there can be no question that the British Isles are well and truly in Europe; and there is nothing their people can do to make it otherwise. Long before the poisonous waves from Chernobyl, it was obvious that the destruction of our forests and woodlands, the pollution of our seas, and the contamination of our atmosphere, with the consequent effects on both the ozone layer and the air we breathe, had become major items in a long catalogue of environmental issues that crossed too many frontiers for any one country to act alone to put them right.

Environmental issues, however, are not to be placed in a neat watertight compartment, for they flow into every stream of national life. Defence and foreign policy no less than transport, housing, health and agriculture all have a connection. These are all interests we have in common with some other countries. They are circles of interest and there are many of them. What this book tries to show is that it is only when a circle of interest is made that the countries inside it should attempt some form of common action. A convergence of interests is the one and only ground for international co-operation.

Britain, for example, is in many circles of interest and as these interests are not all shared with the same countries, their membership varies both in size and composition. Like France, with her links with francophone Africa, Britain's circles of interest include countries outside Europe as well as inside. On the other hand, those countries of Eastern Europe in search of new relationships as they advance to freedom, are Europe-oriented in their interests, which makes them more readily disposed to participating in circles of co-operation with neighbours in Western Europe. Are we in the West to miss this opportunity to build a buttress to the fragile edifice of democracy in the East?

4

The European Community ought to include most of Europe. As this book seeks to show, there are important matters for the attention of a community of European nations touching not just the Twelve but other countries too. To expect most of these others to submit to supranational control is scarcely realistic. For Switzerland to surrender her unique system of federal government would be, to every Swiss, something quite unthinkable. The people of Sweden are only a little less reluctant, it seems, to change their form of government; and like the Swiss, they wish to protect their neutralist stance, although the Community's treaties say nothing about defence. Norway, far from neutralist, may prove to be too democratically robust to tolerate the remoteness of a supranational authority. As for the new members, Greece, Spain and Portugal, despite the massive sums of largesse flowing from Brussels in their direction, they are showing signs of irritation at some of the decisions that also come. And what of Poland, Hungary and Eastern Germany? Having cut their chains, will their appetite for self-government be assuaged by Brussels?

The EC, as it is now, works on the assumption that for its member countries, there is only one circle of interest. This is its weakness. Quite apart from the experience of the last twenty years of too many internal conflicts, the assumption makes it too difficult for the Community to satisfy the concerns of a membership enlarged to include the majority of the people of Europe without injuring minorities that may number many millions. It is too big, yet too small. It is too big to have regard to the interests of minorities, and too small to embrace those problems which may pervade the whole of Europe. A little place called Chernobyl has shown us that though Europe may consist of over thirty countries, it is getting smaller as we come near to the demands and pressures that will arise in the twenty-first century.

This book is a plea for the EC to adopt the international approach and abandon the supranational. Its record over the last thirty years may make us wonder whether supranationalism is the way to coax ancient nation-states, with peoples not given to cast aside too lightly their chauvinistic instincts to come together in harmony. "A nation", said Lord Palmerston, "has no friends, only interests". It was his view that a nation, the aggregate of millions, cannot liken itself to an individual man or woman capable of an emotional affinity, the basis of friendship, with another. Whether one nation lives in peace with another depends upon its interests. If their interests converge, cordial relations, even harmony, will ensue naturally, and the ground is laid for a common policy to cement together the common interest.

There were many common interests among the founding members of the EC. Twelve is inescapably twice six, and the divergence of interests among the Twelve is likely to be more than twice as many as it was among the original Six. The Twelve, by including one neutralist country, the Republic of Ireland, makes it impossible to secure a common defence policy in the EC, and that is far from being the only example of a circle of interest which fails to coincide with the circle of the Twelve. Indeed, within the Twelve there are as many circles of interest as there are circles which include some of the Twelve and take in others outside their number. Therefore, once the Treaty of Rome set the Community on the path of supranationalism, some measure of discordancy was bound to follow. More than three decades have passed since it was signed. An assessment is overdue of how effective its supranational principles have been. This would be incomplete without a glance at the kind of people who have done so much to set a large part of Europe on this supranational path.

In Western Europe there have been several thousand

men and women working to make a dream come true. The dream is of a United States of Europe or the submergence of nation-states into a federal union. They include many of the officials employed in the EC Commission, some distinguished journalists and commentators in our quality newspapers, leading academics at our universities and prominent industrialists. Seldom are they explicit about this dream, for they acknowledge that the great majority of the people of Western Europe are averse to it; as one of them said to me, "the ordinary people are atavistically nationalistic." Their good intentions need not be questioned. Some of them believe nation-states are the intrinsic cause of war. Others that only a super-state, with its economies of scale, can provide the conditions for a dynamic economy. The motives of the captains of the multinational companies may be a little different. How irritating for them it must be to argue and negotiate with twelve different legislatures, each with different concerns and different procedures, when the job of protecting their own interests can be equally well achieved by persuading just one lot of officials in Brussels. Not only that, to be able to move the companies' capital, management team and factories to wherever it is most profitable, without being fettered by national controls, is a huge advantage, especially when it is necessary to challenge a smaller company rooted in one particular part of just one nation-state.

Those mega-businessmen apart, one finds the federalists kindly people; but though we need throw no stones at their good faith, it is time to heed their tactics, and especially it is important to note the steps they advocate towards federal union. The United States of Europe can only come by degrees, every few years another move made towards the goal, but each move is selected so that there is no means of going back. Each is thus like a ratchet movement. The unwary citizens — which

7

includes the overwhelming majority of MPs — agree to each move forward towards federal union, not because it is seen as such, but for some plausible and pragmatic reason. Why did a majority of the House of Commons vote in favour of a directly elected European Assembly? It was to make the Community a little more democratic and to bring decision-making closer to the people, which was manifestly a desirable move and difficult to challenge. The federalists never uttered a word about their objective of a supranational Parliament to which the House of Commons would be made subordinate. That done, the next move was to change the official name of the European Assembly and make it a Parliament. It was, we were told, generally called a parliament and the change would avoid confusion. The steps to a common currency are likewise urged on purely pragmatic grounds.

The idea of European citizenship is also coming in gradually and, cynics might say, with stealth. The laws of immigration are becoming harmonised — for pragmatic reasons, they would say — but they have an essential bearing upon citizenship. Each country in the EC is now persuaded to introduce a new kind of passport. How this helps immigration officers is not entirely plain unless it is suspected that some of them, as they sit at the point of control, flipping through an endless number of pass-ports, are not to be relied upon to remember which country is or is not in the Community. To the holders of the passports it is perhaps intended to have a symbolic rather than practical effect. It helps him or her to feel European and to edge towards a different kind of citizenship. To carry with one, wherever one goes abroad, a means of identification which has an essential similarity to what, for example a German and a Belgian have in their possession as they travel in a foreign country will naturally have an assimilative effect in identifying oneself with others.

Together with that psychological outcome, which naturally appeals to the federalist and perhaps to the rest of us, there is an important legal and constitutional impact. The passport is the citizen's protection. In the case of the UK passport, the Queen's government calls upon other governments to protect its holder because the holder has given and owes allegiance to the Queen. The protection afforded is conditional upon that allegiance. This may seem arcane, if not academic, but it is neither of those things in time of war. William Joyce was an Irishman who travelled to Germany on the eve of the Second World War with the aid of a UK passport and subsequently broadcast to the British people in malapert tones over the ether which earned him the title of Lord Haw-Haw. The legal significance of his passport, far from being academic, became a matter of his life and death. In fact, it hanged him. Tried for treason at the Old Bailey, his guilt turned upon whether he owed allegiance to the King. As an Irishman he claimed to be an alien, but having acquired a UK passport and taken advantage of the protection it gave, he had actively taken a step which formed the basis of a contract, and his allegiance was thus inferred.

Since then four decades of peace have faded the legal significance of a passport, but even a lesser conflict in the future could bring it to the fore again. What happens, then, to a citizen of Europe? Once the contract between the Queen and citizen goes, so must the bond between them be loosened. The federalist will say that the European Community, being a power greater than the UK, will be able to give greater protection to the individual citizen. That may be true, but the truth will depend upon a great deal of power moving from the Queen's government, and of the governments of all the other member countries, to the European Community, transforming it

9

into a powerful mega-state.

Some believe that there are already too many super-powers in the world and that they are inherently a danger to peace, being almost by definition too powerful for ordinary men and women to influence. If by democracy we mean the diffusion of power — and Abraham Lincoln's famous description of democracy is simply another way of saying power should be diffused — it seems very difficult to reconcile the principles of democracy with the concentration of power that goes with a mega-state.

It is important to be clear about the difference between a mega-state and a federal union. In the latter, the constituent states, in theory although seldom in practice, retain their own identities. There has to be a constitution providing for checks and balances between them and the union, setting limits to the powers of each. The federal authorities must also be directly responsible to the people for whom they enact laws and from whom they collect taxes; and the dilemma here is that as the federation grows larger its authorities become more remote from the people they govern, while the influence of any elector or body of electors diminishes to vanishing point. This is clearly a danger in Europe as the EC enlarges to take in new states.

But the greater danger for Europe is that it will become a mega-state, when most people do not even want it to go as far as becoming a federation. Most of the books written in favour of Britain being in the European Community were prompted by dreams of a federal union, a United States of Europe, but with a few honourable exceptions their authors hid this from their readers.

Much of this story has been told in Uwe Kitzinger's *Diplomacy and Persuasion: How Britain Joined the Common Market, 1973*. It is an honest and candid account of how a small group of federalists, just six in number, came together after the Second World War to plan and to plot how their dream could come true.

Among the most influential of these books by the federalists was *Britain and the new Europe* published in 1962 and written by Michael Shanks and John Lambert. They were probably the first to show that there were four elements needed to achieve a unified and integrated political union. A common fiscal policy is obviously one of them, for unless there is a common system of taxation with the same principles applied throughout, and broadly similar rates, obvious distortions of the market will follow. Also various interventionist mechanisms such as exchange controls, import controls and controls over prices and incomes, each essentially a government interference with one price or another, must be the same in all parts of the Common Market. Monetary policy is the third element insofar as governments use interest rates as a means of controlling the economy. The fourth is the control of exchange rates, a powerful weapon in the hands of any government.

In a chapter entitled "Towards a United States of Europe", the authors showed that once those four powers were transferred from the national government to the supranational authority, a United States of Europe was *de facto* in existence. Together those four powers of control are weapons of unassailable strength; once they are surrendered each member country ceases to manage its own economy. As soon as this control of the economy passes, almost everything else of consequence follows suit; for what a government spends on health, transport, education, defence, social welfare, police and prisons — indeed on anything — is decided by the strength of its economy and the system of taxation.

The authors' scenario suggested that the British people would be taken gently towards a federal Europe as if on a raft drifting down a river inexorably with the

11

current. To tell the British people as they got on the raft that they were going to a federal Europe would make them instantly leap off in fear and panic. As it is, two of those four powers have effectively passed out of the hands of the British government. The reason why the federalists are so anxious for the United Kingdom to join fully the European Monetary System is that the other two powers would then silently go, too.

Although the essential argument is said to be between those who desire a deeper Europe and those less ambitious mortals who believe in a wider Europe, it may prove to be more complicated than that. So far as some of the nations are concerned, they may well wish to go deeper in their association with neighbours. The Benelux countries are a case in point. There are circles of interest on the Continent that can well justify a great degree of depth or even total integration. But it is difficult to see how this will apply to all of the Twelve.

Chapter 2 shows how there are two roads to go, and only two, for nation-states when they want to work together. So the essential argument is more about which road we should take, the supranational or the international. For Europe, the supranational road will lead either to a mega-state or to some kind of federal structure with power centralised. The international road will be travelled along by the countries of Europe willing to associate together to co-ordinate their activities in what I have called "circles of overlapping interest".

Not until this question is settled does it seem wise to contemplate matters of width or depth. For the Community with its existing or any larger membership, this book seeks to show that the supranational approach is inappropriate. Once set aside it will enable the Community to open its doors to the rest of Europe. It could then evolve into an open Europe where any country may participate if it believes its interests converge with others, but stands aside when its interests are otherwise. The European Community could then be open in another sense. Today, its commercial and agricultural policies are founded upon the principle of Community Preference. It means that people living within the Community must be coaxed, by taxes, tariffs and other protectionist measures, to prefer what is produced from within the Community rather than have the wider freedom of choice in the world market. The principle is inherently selfish and it has blatantly done much damage to the Third World, as well as weakening the Western Alliance. Were the Community to be refashioned into a free trade area instead of a customs union, commercial links throughout the whole of Europe would become more feasible and, as Chapter 6 shows, do less damage both to world trade and to consumer welfare. Each member state would then be set at liberty to enter into whatever agreements with third countries it wished.

This brings us to the question of sovereignty. It is a term that causes much obfuscation, for no language on the Continent has a word with precisely the same meaning. The French speak of *souveraineté*, the Germans of *souveränität*, the Italians of *sovranita* and the Spanish of *suberanta*. They mean dominion or hegemony or the power of the state. Sovereignty, however, is a term well understood by constitutional lawyers in the English speaking world, being the sum total of the coercive powers once exercised absolutely by the sovereign of England over the people, which in the course of history have come to be shared with the second and third estates of the realm. It is so-called because it attaches to the sovereign. Today we like to say the sovereign powers have passed to the people, or at least to their representatives, so that the British have become a sovereign people. The powers are fivefold, as Chapter 2 explains. But for most people in their daily lives the important ones are

13

the powers to tax and to legislate.

In the European Community, it is said, sovereignty is not lost but pooled. This may be true if we mean it in the sense that politicians speak of it on the Continent. It is not true if we mean sovereignty in the sense constitutionalists use the word in the English language. When William I, let us remember, conquered England he did so in every sense. Every square foot of England's soil became his personal property, its people his subjects, and he appropriated the exclusive right to make and interpret all its laws and levy all its taxes. Since then, many thousands of people have died, been tortured or imprisoned to take that sovereignty away, because they believed sovereignty was not being exercised in their interests. The sovereignty so gained can be pooled but, as many Scotsmen, Welshmen and Irishmen will confirm, this pooling is satisfactory only when there is a convergence of interests with the others with whom it is pooled. As the number of people governed in one unit gets larger, so does the danger of a minority interest being overlooked; and that, of course, is the principal benefit of living in a small country. So the more nations adhere to the common system of law or taxation, the more dangerous it becomes for minorities. Moreover, a whole nation can become a minority when the sovereignty of several is pooled. All is well if the interests of all the nations happen to be the same, but once they differ, the pooling of sovereignty becomes a source of friction. The larger the number of countries forming a group for any kind of co-operation, the more important it is for each of them to retain its sovereignty, thus being able to withdraw from a policy in order to protect its own interests. This puts the supranationalist into something of a dilemma.

As sovereignty matters when a country's interests are not the same as its neighbours, its pooling if permanent,

14

as it is when transferred to a supranational authority, becomes a dangerous loss. An example of this arose from the common fisheries policy whereby the seas around the British Isles ceased to be British waters and became the Community's. Thousands of fishermen from France, Belgium and other parts of the Community, having depleted their own fishing stocks, were given the right to move into the traditional fishing grounds of the British fishermen. Britain, having lost legislative control (or sovereignty) over her own waters, has been powerless to prevent depletion of her fishing grounds. The consequences for Hull, Grimsby and other fishing ports have been disastrous. From Boston, in my constituency, only two boats now go out instead of thirty-five as used to be the case.

Have we gone too far down the supranational road to change direction now? There are several reasons for believing it is feasible to change, all of them grounded on the fact that the Community as it now stands is not working satisfactorily and will have to change in one way or another.

In the first place, there is what is called the "democratic deficit", a phrase adopted by members of the European Parliament in their quest for legislative and fiscal powers. The laws of the Community are passed by the Council of Ministers, and these, according to the Treaty of Rome, overrule anything decided by the national parliaments. In the form of regulations they take effect immediately and each member country has to enforce them in the same way as the laws passed by its own legislature. Most of the more important Community legislation is in the form of directives, directions to the national parliaments to introduce laws that will be the same in each country. The national parliaments have no alternative but to pass them. They may pretend (as the House of Commons does frequently) that the proposal

15

springs from within; the self-esteem of an ancient parliament must not be hurt; yet it remains something of a charade, for neither the House of Commons nor any of the other parliaments can do anything to the draft legislation except nod approval. There is no power to reject the directive, nor any power to amend it.

Individual governments may have no objection to this procedure, as it is no inconvenience to them. A member of the government has agreed it in the Council of Ministers; that is the general rule, and if he has had to compromise or if it is one of those cases where majority decisions on the Council are permissible and he has been outvoted, as compensation he is likely to get his own way on a subsequent issue. What exactly happens on these occasions, and to what extent a minister has sacrificed a minority interest, is not for us to know. The debates are behind closed doors. What each minister says in this process of law-making is secret, as indeed is every other part of the procedure.

The members of the European Parliament are not slow to make the point that nowhere else in the democratic world are laws passed or taxes imposed in such secrecy. How can the legislators be accountable to the people for what they have done if the people are to have no account of why the laws were passed in that way? The European Parliament can, it is true, give an opinion on forthcoming legislation, but the Council of Ministers is under no obligation to be bound by it and frequently proceeds without first receiving an opinion.

Much of our law has already been changed by this clandestine procedure; and although some minorities have been injured, for example when lorry weights were increased, there has yet to be felt a dramatic impact upon the people of any of the member countries. However, this will certainly come with the single market and the widespread introduction of majority voting in the Coun-

cil of Ministers. Eighty per cent of the economic and
social decisions now made by the national parliaments
will, in the view of the President of the Commission, be
then taken in Brussels. Even allowing for a fifty per cent
error by him, the consequences will be immense,
extending into every segment of what is important
economically and socially.

To have these far-reaching decisions about our lives
made by the Council of Ministers behind closed doors
will be intolerable. To have them made publicly by the
European Parliament by men and women directly elected and accountable to their constituents is an obvious
alternative. I hope the last chapter shows what a sham
that would be. For one man or woman, who must of
necessity spend several days a week in Westminster, to be
accountable to 60,000 or 70,000 is difficult enough; for
him or her to represent and be accountable to seven or
eight times that number is deep in the realm of the
impossible. Europe with democracy, as this book seeks
to show, is a Europe of many sovereign parliaments.

Historians have shown us why empires and power *blocs*
never last for long; and the longer they survive the more
devastating the consequences when disintegration
comes. They are too big to be on a human scale and anything that is found for some reason to be too big has
within it an element of self-destruction. One body will
not naturally cohere with another, for every single cell
has what Spinoza called *conatus*, that striving for survival
as an independent entity. Animals have it more than
microbes; a territorial imperative magnifies the *conatus*,
and a will to rise in the pecking order adds a little spice to
the mixture. With human beings, spurred on by a host of
ambitions attainable in a modern society, not least of all
the urge for the esteem of others in a variety of ways, this
conatus can be measurably greater. When found in an
aggregate of humans, we call it nationalism, patriotism

or chauvinism, depending upon their motives or our prejudices. Whether the separate units are bits of physical matter, animals or human beings, the same principle applies — there is no integration unless there is a natural coherence. The herd instinct may be there, but only when each in the herd has the urge to belong, which can only spring from a sense of interdependence. Is this sense of interdependence so strong among 320 million people of Western Europe that to satisfy their *conatus* they must merge together and be as one nation in nearly all matters of moment?

When fainthearts murmur it is too late to halt the march of the Community, they echo what was said no doubt by the Ancient Britons when they saw the Romans building Hadrians's Wall; it was said no doubt again within a few years or even a few months of the demise of the Roman Empire; and yet again by the Lavals and Quislings when Hitler's New Economic Order was planted on their soil (and, incidentally, a study of the details of that Order is rather interesting as we approach the single market).   One reason why a change of direction by the Community is feasible follows from its need for revenue; and in this respect the UK's membership is all-important. The UK and Western Germany being the two main paymasters of the Community, it would collapse without their money. Western Germany can, however, justify the largesse to her neighbours on two grounds. Her expenditure on defence is very modest in relation to her GDP, and can remain so while the US and the UK take on the burden; at least it enables her to make a generous contribution to the Community funds. Secondly, she is the one country in the EC which has gained most from a tariff-free access to the Common Market.

Before the UK joined the Common Market her tariffs against the other member-countries were appreciably higher than theirs. Once they were removed, a trade imbalance began and has since continued to get worse. Before the UK entered the Common Market, exports and imports across the English Channel were usually in balance and any advantage was in the UK's favour. Since then, the other countries have gradually stepped up their exports to the UK with no corresponding increase in imports from the UK: Britain has therefore become the largest export market for France, and almost the largest for Western Germany. Thus the UK now imports manufactured goods from the rest of the Community that are worth £10,000 million more than she exports to the other countries. It has been estimated as being the equivalent of one million jobs lost.

The gravity of this imbalance has been masked by the export of North Sea oil. Once this begins to decline the consequences will be most serious. At the root of it is the fact that the UK has a large industrial population at the periphery of the market. Other countries on the periphery, such as Ireland, Portugal, Greece and Denmark have small populations and are still mainly agricultural. The midlands and north of England will have the same experience in the integrated single market as the north of Scotland, Ireland and most of Wales when the integrated market of the United Kingdom was formed many years ago and subsequently developed by modern transport. So long as the UK remains one of the paymasters, her powers of persuasion are not to be underestimated. Nor would the other industrialised members of the Community wish to see barriers erected against them in the soft market which is Britain. No country is better placed than Britain to coax the Community into change.

Do we need new institutions for the wider Europe? The Conference on Security and Co-operation in Europe has been canvassed as one whose shadowy existence should be given some substance. It has the merit of being

19

supported by thirty-five countries, but so has the Economic Commission for Europe, which has the added advantage of an existing establishment in Geneva, besides a record of achievement in securing many successful schemes of Europe-wide co-operation. To give the CSCE a revived role may be useful, but its potential competence can scarcely compare with that of the ECE. Better than both would be the European Community, open to all European peoples with one important proviso. It is this: that it recognises that the sovereign powers of making the laws or levying the taxes for all the peoples of Europe are too important both for them and for the good of democracy to be centralised in a single distant city, just one of Europe's thirty-five capitals.

1

Europe: Twelve or Many More?

Whether the European Community becomes deeper or
wider is a question somewhat clouded over by a new
word much used in the debate — subsidiarity. What
individual nations can do best for themselves should be
done by them; those are the subsidiary matters; and only
what they cannot do best for themselves need be done by
the Community. This congenial principle does not help
us answer two crucial questions. The first is: how should
the nations of Europe act together? As the next chapter
shows, there are only two roads for the nations to travel
together, supranationally or internationally, and until it
is decided which of the two is likely to bring the greater
concord, little will be achieved of lasting value. The
second question is no less important. If it is true that
there are occasions when nations must work together
with agreed common policies, how do we decide which
nations are to be included or excluded? Does some
supranational authority, set above the national governments, decree that Whiteland and Blueland are unable to

do something for themselves, while Blackland and Redland can do so and should therefore be excluded? Is it so unreasonable to believe that Blackland and Redland both have governments capable of making up their own minds as to what they can do for their own countries?

This brings us at once to the size of the European Community. Is it to be an exclusive club of Twelve? This will make it difficult to reconcile it with the principle of subsidiarity, for if it acts supranationally as it does now, it assumes that all twelve member states must act as one whenever there is an occasion when they cannot do something effectively on their own. It presupposes that the Twelve are a homogeneous entity. More difficult to believe is the assumption that a neighbouring state does not share the same concerns. The exclusive club of Twelve is the natural objective of anyone who desires the Community to evolve into a unitary mega-state, another super-power, which throws its weight around as an expression of Western Europe's post-imperial dreams. As such it will be singularly ill-equipped to overcome some of the urgent problems listed in another chapter that are beginning to face all corners of Europe.

Also among those who want the Twelve to be an exclusive club are the people still fearful of an invasion by the Soviet Union. They find comfort behind the barriers, for they still see a vision of Russian hordes one day sweeping across central Europe until they eventually march through the gates of Buckingham Palace. As that scenario remains possible in the minds of some policy makers, we might ask ourselves whether a Community of Twelve, gradually becoming itself a federal union or mega-state would pose a threat to the peace of mind of the Soviet leaders and so be a target for the kind of subversion at which the agents of the Soviet Union have proved themselves so adept. A United States of Europe or European Union, whose people enjoyed political freedom as well as economic prosperity, within the same continent as the Soviet Union, despite the new void of central Europe, would do more to frighten the Kremlin than the siting of 1000 nuclear missiles.

How, then, would they see the alternative of an open and wider Europe? By placing an emphasis on the environmental problems of Europe — the geographer's Europe, that is — all the governments east of the Elbe would see an advantage to be gained. Writing in the *New European* in the summer issue, 1988, Mr. Valentin Falin, a prominent member of the Central Committee in the Soviet Union and a long-standing colleague of Mr. Gorbachev, spoke of Europe having less than ten years to solve some of its environmental problems: unless they were solved, Europe would destroy herself. Mr. Falin gave his readers to understand that this was not merely his own view, but one shared by others in power in the Soviet Union.

None of the Russian leaders see themselves as Asiatics; indeed they appear to show some disdain for what is beyond the Urals. Tolstoy's literature, they say, belongs to Europe no less than Shakespeare's (and from all accounts they more avidly read the latter) and Tchaikovsky's symphonies are Europe's as much as Beethoven's. What the Communist Party is permitting in the Soviet Union — the devolution of power and the private ownership of homes, land and even small businesses, and the lifting of censorship — is evidence that the failure of an ideology is a least partly recognised. A European Community that enables them to join and enter the circles of common interest could do much to support those changes. Sitting together at the conference table when it is in one's interests to agree is in itself conducive to a better understanding between people hitherto suspicious of one another; and when followed, as it always appears to be, by eating and drinking together, a bond may replace a barrier. A succession of such conferences, as would be the case, involving a variety of different ministers and advisers, ought to go a long way to removing fear between the two halves of Europe. And if it also helped the Soviet leaders to shed a little more of their ideology, so much the better.

Europe is not now, any more than she ever has been, some homogeneous entity; and, pray God, may she never be. To speak of any one thing embracingly as "European" is to risk putting a shadow upon the glory of Europe which stems and flows from her very diversity. Europe, it has been said, is rather a tapestry of no design, each piece added without a preconceived plan, but once completed giving the eye a blaze of dazzling colours. After all, Europe is so diverse and has so many different countries, that it is difficult to say with any certainty how many there are. *The International Year Book* lists thirty-five while omitting Andorra, San Marino and Liechtenstein, and while counting the European Republics in the Soviet Union as one.

Whether Europe consists of twelve, thirty-five or even more countries, there is not one of them that can afford to stay outside all the different circles of interest. These circles can be positioned in two different ways. The advocates of a deeper Europe speak of concentric circles. An inner core consists of the Twelve; next to them are the members of EFTA; and beyond them the remaining countries of Europe:

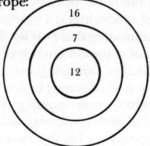

The Twelve are not just at the core of the Community, but are the very heart where all decisions are made, even for the Seven who join to form the Economic Space. As for the remaining sixteen, they seem to acquire a third class place, with as yet no defined role except the hint that some sort of association agreement may be reached. Brussels being at the centre, the thrust of co-operation implies the centrification of power. Not unnaturally this has its attractions for the Franco-German partnership.

The alternative is an indefinite number of circles that are overlapping, like the symbol of the Olympics:

Each circle represents an interest. These interests are matters in which governments intervene but recognise that they cannot satisfy their national interests unless they co-operate with one or more other governments. Trade and defence, ever since governments began, have been two such circles of interest. In the context of Europe, the maximum advantage to its people would be gained if every country were in the circle of trade, but no-one would claim that in present circumstances the same applies in the case of defence. The twentieth century has seen the list of these interests lengthened to an indefinite number. Some of them are set out in a subsequent chapter.

What is important is that this alternative has not the rigidity of concentric circles. These circles will vary in size; for example the Benelux countries may wish to be as one over some matters; on the periphery only a few countries will decide to be part of a circle. Nor should these circles be always limited to Europe. However, the principle of self-determination should be paramount, so that each country can determine for itself whether to co-operate with others.

For several reasons this alternative might be called a Europe of democratic circles. If it is true that politics is about how governments ought to make decisions concerning the hopes and fears of people, then it is pellucidly clear that Abraham Lincoln's three elements of democracy are not to be forgotten. In M. Delors' Europe of concentric circles, there may be government of the people and for the people, but scarcely any claim of government by the people when the 320 million in the inner circle are to be treated as a homogeneous entity whose interests are one and the same and when the 200 millions in the middle and outer circles are not intended to have any direct representation in the decision-making. Diffusion of power is the essence of democracy; no society can be more democratic than a small village community with a population so homogeneous that it is able to decide its affairs with harmonious unanimity. Once power moves away to a centre remote from the people and seen in their eyes to be remote, democracy is in retreat. The concentration of power is the hallmark of empire; and if concentric circles are to be made around Brussels, some may be tempted to speak of a Europe of imperial circles.

A common policy succeeds only when it stems from a common interest. That is trite, yet there is little if anything in common between the farmers in Greece and Sicily and those in Connemara and Shetland; between the countries of the Mediterranean and those of northern Europe a great gulf has been fixed by nature herself and no common policy will be devised to harmonise the soil, climate and terrain, and so enable a single common policy to succeed for all western Europe's agriculture. Another example concerns the great rivers of the Danube and the Rhine. Both are polluted; and it is in the interests of the countries through which they pass that steps be taken to curb the pollution. A common policy might cost a great deal of money to put into effect and to enforce subsequently. Though river pollution is a problem of European dimensions, it would be singularly unjust to expect the tax-payers of, say, Ireland or Denmark or Greece to contribute to the cost; nor are the interests of the Germans alongside the Rhine the same as the interests of the Austrians alongside the Danube. Far better, therefore, for individual policies to be devised for each of these great rivers; common laws or regulations would then be passed for each country affected and, if public expenditure were needed, the necessary revenue could be raised by agreement. Just as we need a means for all the countries of Europe to come together for a particular purpose, so we need — and probably more so — a means whereby some of them may not do so. Pollution of the Rhine may concern four or five countries; the Danube six; and in either case their interests could be served by some institution of Europe to initiate and coordinate the steps necessary to overcome the problem.

Another reason to doubt the concentric circle approach is confirmed by many who have negotiated in the Council of Ministers. To secure the agreement of all the member states to a common policy intended to benefit only a few of them, a great deal of horse-trading has to be done. France, Germany and the Netherlands want the EC to put right the pollution of the Rhine, and not unnaturally to pay for it. To get the others to agree they offer to help the United Kingdom and Italy over some matter in which they have an interest. Then the smaller member states think they are being imposed upon, so they too have to be given something. Schemes for the spending of money are decided not on their merits, still less because of some urgent need, but to make sure that the taxpayers in another country are satisfied that, solving the problems of others, they also will receive some benefits. The outcome of it all is that the final decision becomes a packet of morsels which tries to give something to everyone. So a sludgy amalgam eventually comes into being, and the merits of the original proposal may disappear from view.

The supranationalist brushes aside this obstacle to cost-effectiveness; he looks across the Atlantic and sees a model constitution. The United States of America as a federal union of states can be for Europe a mirror-image. Others say that as we do not know and cannot tell what will be the final form of "Europe", we must proceed pragmatically, step by step, towards greater unity, and though we may emulate the United States of America in some respects, we may travel differently in others. This view sounds plausible yet, as the next chapter shows, it is the consequence of failing to understand how ancient nation states are able to act in unison. Europe, the continent of so many countries, is not homogeneous, and because it is not so it is to be admired all the more. There is no part of the world of similar size where there is such a richness of diversity. Conservationists will say that conservation of wildlife depends upon diversity. Here is an analogy to be drawn for us in Europe. Thousands of the world's wild flowers only flourish in conditions of low fertility; they die if moved from the bleakness of a mountainside or the sparseness of heathland or the impoverished soil of downland. Some want a tropical climate, others a temperate; some the terrain of wet-lands, others the Alps. Unless conditions are diverse, so that each plant, and each animal, too, can find the environment it needs for its survival, the conservationists lose the struggle. Standardised, harmonised, universally regulated conditions are the very death. Just as they destroy what the conservationists want to conserve, so they can destroy the rich diversity of European life.

This sum total of diversity has given Europe values that vary from country to country; and the rest of the world has drawn heavily from them, picking out those it prefers while discarding others. If Charlemagne had secured the aim of a united European empire would John Locke have been born generations later a free man, and would his liberal philosophy have been written down to influence future generations? Perhaps, by the time he came into the world, Charlemagne's empire would have collapsed, but for as long as it had lasted it would have quelled the growth of liberal learning and smothered the seeds that later flowered with Locke. Napoleon, too, saw the vision of a united Europe; had he won at Waterloo, would John Stuart Mill have written *On Liberty?* The fact that these two, Charlemagne and Napoleon, were dictators of a kind and we now speak of a united Europe founded upon democratic principles is beside the point. Whatever form a united Europe takes, whether Hitlerite or democratic, a concentration of power must ensue. Unless power passes from individual nation states, the vision vanishes as surely as the Cheshire cat. Once the power moves away to the capital of the federal union, uniformity must follow. Italian opera goes on as before; Beethoven is still played and French litera-ture is still read almost everywhere; the concentration of power in the new-found capital does not change them nor limit their appeal, nor does it do anything else disagreeable to what has already been achieved in giving the world the values of Europe. But if the process of uniformity begins, the unity of Europe, if it means anything at all, means a sense of one-ness. Italian opera may give more pleasure than any other, so too Beethoven's symphonies and French literature, but they are as they are because life has been different in three adjoining countries. Italian opera was born not for the reason that several men of similar talents were coincidentally born in the same part of Italy; it was the epitome, almost the essence, of all things Italian. The sound of French literature being read is a delight to the ear: one reason is that the French have been willing to submit to a discipline in the use of words that English writers would never have tolerated. But the British people can claim a magnificent output of liberal thought; it has crossed the Atlantic to gain still greater strength, and is now an imperishable beacon to light the way for countless millions.

It is sometimes said that only where there is material prosperity can these good values emerge. The great palaces and cathedrals, the architecture which can influence that of the modest dwelling, would never have been built in times of poverty; fine music needs concert halls of magnificence; and, besides, all art and culture needs patronage of rich men or a rich state; and, whichever it is, there is more money about when society is prospering. Is this entirely true? Charles Dickens might deny that he would have written as he did unless moved by his experiences of abject poverty and human hatred. Most of our poets and many of our artists have conceived their finest works in a state of penury. Whether the jazz of New Orleans ranks as great art may be mooted, but indisputably it was born of suffering and oppression, becoming a joy to millions. As with the conservation of wildlife, the conditions of poverty and barrenness are needed to create diversity; and the poverty and oppression in many parts of Europe have given us some of the values we now cherish the most. Of the many examples which come to mind, let one be enough to prove the point: the "second best book in the English language", *Pilgrim's Progress*, was written by a man in an English prison. Would a latter-day John Bunyan, unfettered and free, have poured out such prose? Few books in any language have had such a lasting impact on the lives of so many people; and probably no book, other than the Bible itself, has been translated into so many languages. Its effect has been incalculable. To one man's afflictions and to the conditions of his time, not least the intolerance and oppression then prevailing, do we owe what he gave to us. This is not to say that gifted young men coming down with a First in English should be made to do a stint at Wormwood Scrubs; to contrive conditions of adversity would be self-defeating; equally, to strive for uniformity must diminish the conditions in which diversity can flourish.

Yet, despite that diversity, we can go through every function of government, even the least important, and we find that in nearly every case there is an advantage to be gained by one country co-ordinating its policies to some extent with others. The smaller the country, the greater the advantage there usually is. To isolate twelve countries from their neighbours and restrict joint action to them alone is to put a ball and chain upon their feet. Europe being a continent of many countries, and most of them quite small, there can be few problems that any of them have which cannot in some way be easier to solve with the co-operation of at least one neighbour.

2

Only Two Roads To Go

Throughout most of the 20th century a succession of writers and academics have purveyed a certain distaste for the nation-state. Much of what they have said can be expressed in the syllogism: nation-states cause wars; wars are bad; therefore, nation-states are bad. Arnold Toynbee, perhaps the most notable of this school of thought, overlooked how every major nation-state has at some stage been plunged into civil war. It is, moreover, these nation-states which tend to declare war themselves; smaller ones do not. It is the relative size and strength of a nation-state that determines whether it can be prone to warmongering. To condemn all nation-states on this ground is to be extraordinarily unfair on, say, Sweden or Switzerland. There is nothing inherent in a nation-state that makes it inclined to invade a neighbour. It is when big nation-states are alongside smaller and weaker neighbours that the danger may be seen. Every new mega-state born is potentially another threat to peace.

The other complaint is that the nation-state is

obsolete, a relic of an age when countries could be gloriously isolationist and self-sufficient. This, too, seems rather harsh upon Sweden and Switzerland. The latter especially is a striking example of a country of high technology with her products traded in all parts of the world, yet she still remains very decidedly a nation-state with no ill-effects and no intention of surrendering her status. What may be wrong with a nation-state, as with every other organised entity, is its size. Mischief is often done by a nation-state, but only by those bigger and more powerful than the ones who suffer the mischief. A nation-state is really no more than a unit of self-government. When a group of these units desire to work together to achieve a common objective, they have two, and only two, ways of doing it. They can proceed internationally or supra-nationally. Any third way is precluded by the characteristics of a nation-state.

It is important, therefore, to spell out these characteristics. Constitutional and international lawyers have for long been agreed that they are:

(i)   the power to make all its own laws;
(ii) the power to interpret its laws in its own courts;
(iii) the power to fix and collect all its taxes;
(iv) the power to declare war;
(v)   the power to make a binding treaty.

As characteristics of the nation-state, they have one feature in common: they are all coercive. The nation-state is able to exercise those five powers because the individual is coerced into acquiescence, either willingly by a majority in a democracy, when the executive, legislature and judicature can between them make those powers effective, or in a totalitarian state, where power is concentrated elsewhere and the acquiescence may be less willing. Whether democratic or totalitarian, once its power of coercion is gone, the nation-state becomes something different, for effectively the sovereign powers themselves have disappeared. Sovereignty is the sum total of those five powers; and for that reason there might be a better understanding of the concept of a nation-state if we used the terms "sovereign nation" or "sovereign people" instead.

Does it really matter if some of those powers of sovereignty or even all of them are transferred to a supranational authority? Of the 159 member countries of the UN, a majority were not eligible to join when the organisation was founded; they had yet to acquire their sovereignty; and having acquired it, often with bloodshed, they show little hint of any ardent desire to surrender it. Each one of these new nation-states is changing from what it was as a colony or mandated territory, and each is changing in a different way. The different changes are coming about because each is exercising its sovereign powers in a way that is different from the others. Nigeria and Ghana, for example, as British colonies, were treated and governed in much the same way; and although there were differences between them then, they were nothing compared with what one may see visibly in Nigeria and Ghana today. Laws change our behaviour: either we obey them so that we act differently or we disobey them and become criminals. So, too, with taxes: their purpose is to make us spend our money differently. The sum total of our laws and taxes decides almost everything of any consequence that we do in our lives. Over a period of time our laws and taxes cause our structure of society to change and to be in one shape rather than another, and to cause our ethical code to include what other nation-states may deplore and exclude what they may tolerate. From the power-house that makes the laws and fixes taxation goes out a host of currents causing waves to ebb and flow into everything we call our way of life. Those members of the chattering classes who dismiss sovereignty as a trifling concern seem to know very little of the influences that guide our conduct. "We must look forward," said Soren Kierkegaard, "but understand backwards." Many centuries in which laws have been made and taxes fixed have given us a long chain of cause and effect which will change and mould the character of the people.

This changing and moulding is done by external influence in the case of a colony or country submitting to a supranational authority; it is done internally, that is by the people themselves, only in a nation-state. This is what J. S. Mill meant when he wrote approvingly of self-government. No matter how benevolently the external power may be exercised, it is better that the people themselves should decide how they should be changed and moulded, i.e. that they should be a sovereign people. That is why it seems that Poles and Hungarians wish to live once again in a nation-state; and those who dismiss nation-states as a "cause of war" or as "obsolete" might consider what advice they should give to the Poles and Hungarians about their aspirations.

It is not easy to think of an example of when a nation has given away any of those five sovereign powers except at the end of a war, a vanquished nation-state capitulating to a victor. When the Allies, in the Second World War decreed the unconditional surrender of Hitler's Germany, they put in two words what a constitutional lawyer would have expressed in twenty times as many. But most surrenders are completed by a treaty, an agreement between states exerting the power of a nation-state. Most of our erstwhile colonies were gained by a treaty; whether some of the tribal chiefs who signed the treaties presided over a nation-state is doubtful, but it did not matter as each side recognised the treaty-making power of the other.

In the present century treaties have been made by the score; and only a few of them have followed a war. It is probably true that no country in the world has entered into more of them than the United Kingdom. In fact, it is difficult to catalogue them all, so many of them have there been. Certainly the list establishes Britain's claim to be as internationally minded as any other country. Until the Treaty of Accession was signed on behalf of the UK on joining the EC, all the treaties made were international. They were *between* nation-states. They were revocable, every one of them. And they surrendered none of the constitutional powers Britain had as a nation-state. The British people made their own laws; they were still interpreted and enforced in British courts; a British Parliament still levied all the taxes and all the revenue went into a national Exchequer; Britain still could make treaties with others; and Britain still could declare war upon another nation.

None of the treaties we entered into put a curb upon how we might exercise the five constitutional powers, nor was it intended that they should do so. One purpose of our signing the treaty that brought into being the United Nations was obviously to avoid another war; a member nation minded to declare war agreed to abide by certain rules before doing so, but this did not prevent many wars breaking out between member nations. The agreement reached at Bretton Woods to launch the International Monetary Fund was intended to regulate the way member states fixed their exchange rates, but floating rates have not been stopped. The General Agreement on Tariffs and Trade required nation-states not to raise existing tariffs; they may come down but not go up; again, member states have resorted to the non-tariff barrier to get round the rules. The NATO treaty inhibits our independent role in defence; France subscribes to it too, but she asserts her independence and others do not demur. In the case of the European Court of Human Rights, Britain's adherence rests on a Convention which Parliament can overrule at any time.

However, by the Treaty of Accession, ratified by the European Communities Act, Britain did not enter an international agreement; it was a treaty by which we submitted to a number of supranational authorities. Thus the British people set out on the supranational road to "Europe". Power in respect of some functions of government were surrendered and duly transferred to institutions with supranational authority, to which our own national institutions, such as Parliament and our Courts of Justice, were made subordinate. Although we have parted with only some of our constitutional powers, only one of them remains totally unchanged by the Treaty of Accession: it is the power to make war. As the main prize of "Europe" was to be peace, the omission may be a trifle ironic.

A war may break out in numerous ways: the conflict in the Falklands was an example of an invasion of another territory, ships being sunk and lives lost and all the symptoms of a war which ended with an act of surrender by armed forces. There was not, in fact, a declaration of war by the United Kingdom and formally speaking no war at all. The distinction is of importance because a war once declared can only come to an end when there is an agreement to that effect, when the victor can impose terms upon the vanquished which may include loss of territory and sometimes total subjugation. War being the usual means of bringing the demise of a nation-state, its declaration is a matter of great constitutional significance. If a state is defeated its constitution is torn up; whether governed as a dictatorship or a democracy, henceforth it proceeds as the victor ordains and its people have little choice in the matter. This power to declare war, with all the consequences that can follow, is the first hallmark of a nation-state. A nation-state can declare war or it can transfer its power to declare war to a supranational authority, so that if the latter takes this step, a state of war formally exists for that country. *There are therefore only two ways that war can be declared: there can be no third way.*

Often it is said that our membership of NATO is an intrusion upon "our sovereignty" and this point has frequently been made in debates about our membership of the EC. The North Atlantic Treaty is in constitutional terms no different from scores of other treaties that have been made by a group of countries for their self-defence. Any signatory to it can leave; it is not irrevocably binding and, above all, though an attack upon one country in NATO would be deemed an attack upon them all, it does not follow that a declaration of war is the consequence. No country in joining NATO has surrendered its status as a nation-state, for a declaration of war must still be made by each individual country in accordance with its own constitution. NATO is not a supranational authority, for none of the five powers of a nation-state have been transferred to it.

It is significant, however, that all the other powers that we have had as a nation-state are now subject to some kind of limitation as a result of our entry into the EC.

No longer can we make a treaty concerning trade with a country outside the Community. Article 228 of the Treaty of Rome makes it clear enough:

> 1. Where this Treaty provides for the conclusion of agreements between the Community and one or more States or an international organisation, such agreements shall be negotiated by the Commission. Subject to the powers vested in the Commission in this field, such agreements shall be concluded by the Council, after consulting the Assembly where required by this Treaty.

The second paragraph of this Article states " Agreements concluded under these conditions shall be binding upon the Institutions of the Community and the Member States." The Community means only the European Economic Community, but the Treaties setting up the other two Communities have a similar clause. The negotiations that led to a treaty and the making of it as well as the signing of it are not done internationally but supranationally. If it were done internationally, the representatives of each nation-state would take part in the negotiation on the drafting; and when it came to be signed, it would not be binding unless a signatory from each nation-state made it so. The Treaty of Rome takes all the member states along a supranational road and transfers from the member states to a supranational authority, namely the Commission, the power to negotiate the terms of the agreement. It is true that the Council concludes the agreement and on the Council may be a minister from each member state, but whether majority voting or unanimity prevails, an individual member state cannot step out of line.

Let us see how this transfer of treaty-making powers affects the British people in a simple matter of everyday life. The people who make steak and kidney pies say they want to import from Australia more of the kind of beef that is produced so well there. It is ranch-reared, very lean, with no fat even in the muscle, unlike the beef readily available over here. Their customers prefer that kind of beef, but the piemakers are not allowed to import what they would like from Australia to satisfy their customers. In fact, it is a criminal offence. If a steak and kidney piemaker went to Australia and returned with any extra beef under his arm, our customs officers would have the duty of taking him to one side and charging him with a crime. In due course, assuming that he would be granted bail, he would stand in the dock and be sentenced. Perhaps only a fine would be imposed and that is no great hardship, but if he could not or would not pay the penalty, a term of imprisonment would follow. Loss of liberty is the sanction; the shame of being detained by the police and of being required to stand in a dock where the previous prisoner may have been a murderer or a burglar, together with the publicity in the local newspapers, are threats sufficient to deter most of us. As he sees his shipment of beef taken away by customs officers, his conscience may be clear; and pondering on the perils of doing only what his customers would like him to do, he may exercise the right of every free-born Briton to write to his MP about it. The MP will have a ready answer. *He* did not pass the law making it a crime to bring in a piece of beef for steak and kidney pies; *he* had nothing to do with it. However, had he been in the House of Commons in 1972 and voted for the European Communities Act, he would not be altogether truthful. It was that Act of Parliament which handed over the treaty-making powers to the institutions of the European Community. Unless that deed had been done, the institutions could not have become, for us, supranational authorities. In the matter of treaties with nation-states outside the EC our own national institutions became subordinate to those of the Communities. From 1066 to January 1st 1973, first England and then the United Kingdom entered into hundreds of treaties with other powers; in every case, the signature of or on behalf of the King or Queen was the act that made it binding. Today the signature, the manifestation of sovereignty, is made by a man in Brussels. As a matter of convention rather than of law (for a treaty is an executive not a legislative act) no treaty of importance was signed unless its terms were first debated in the House of Commons; and no Prime Minister or any other minister in the twentieth century put his hand to a document on behalf of Her Majesty's Government unless confident of the support of the British people as expressed in Parliament. Today, when it comes to all

41

matters economic, that act of popular approval resides in the European Parliament. Although elected, they are self-evidently a supranational body: Article 228 of the Treaty of Rome gives them power and authority in respect of treaties which exceed those of the House of Commons.

The negotiating and making of treaties often seem far away from the everyday life of ordinary people. Sometimes this is the case, but treaties or agreements about trade and economic policy have results that can spill into every home in the land. Trade is about what people want to buy — things to have or food to eat — and it concerns economic welfare and the standard of living. The little bits of steak that the British palate prefers in the steak and kidney pie may seem a trifling example of loss of sovereignty, but several hundred similar cases added together come to a major change in a nation's habits and preferences.

Enforced uniformity does not create unity; in fact, it tends to have the opposite effect. Unity, if it is to endure and to stand on firm ground, must come willingly, and the more that different peoples have enjoyed the freedom to be different the more important that willingness becomes. It is a powerful argument against agreements being made for trade or economic policy supranationally, unless they are ratified by the legislatures of the individual member states. The British people, through their own government, cannot enter into an agreement with, say, Japan, for her to export to us cars and television sets (which seem to be rather popular with the British people) free of tariffs or other barriers in return for favourable terms for our financial services, such as insurance, to be exported to Japan, where, it so happens, they are much in demand. Such an agreement might be in the interests of both countries, but though Japan, being a nation-state, is free to enter into such an agreement, the United Kingdom is not.

New Zealand butter is still allowed to enter our ports, but an import levy or tax of about sixty pence a pound has to be paid upon it, otherwise it would sell for about half the price of butter produced in the Common Market. The consumers would buy it if they could, we can be pretty sure, so they have to be stopped from doing so. Therefore an agreement is reached with New Zealand that she sends us no more than a limited tonnage every year. The agreement is not negotiated by the parties principally concerned, for New Zealand producers have the terms of the agreement imposed upon them, and the agreement is made not by a British Government on behalf of the British people, but by the Commission of the EC on behalf of over 300 million in the Community. That the butter is only going to be eaten by the British people is beside the point; their wishes are subsumed into those of the Community. The Commission has entered into a host of other agreements, too. A long catalogue of foodstuffs and other items are affected which we are thus allowed or not allowed to buy.

Two important principles arise. The first is that the Commission naturally takes into account the interest of the 300 million people, but it can only do so in general terms; the interests of minorities have second place, since uniformity prevails. The other principle is even more important. These trade agreements are not to be compared with an ordinary commercial contract. Having the force of a treaty, they can overrule or nullify a contract made between importer and exporter. If it says, "No more than 70,000 tonnes of butter shall be imported from New Zealand", the statement has the force of the law, and it becomes illegal for anyone to import a single ounce more than that. Such an agreement can only be made by an authority with constitutional powers to do so. A nation-state has such powers; so does a supranational authority such as the EC. *There is no third way of making a trading agreement with the force of coercion.*

Trade apart, it is generally accepted that to make the Community work, agreements must be reached between a number of states about quite a long list of subjects. These agreements, whether called treaties or not, will be worthless pieces of paper unless made with an authority with the power to bind the people in each country concerned. No advance towards co-operation can be made until we settle who has the power to do so. Either it is a nation-state or it is an authority to which the power is ceded.

The third hallmark of a nation-state touches taxation. Who decides what is to be taxed, the degree to which it is to be taxed, and how the tax is to be collected? If such powers lie exclusively within a country, it has one of the essential elements of a nation-state; equally, if some part of those powers ceases to reside exclusively within the country, then it has lost this part of its sovereignty. People who brush this aside as a piece of pedantry forget their history. England's history since 1066, let us remember, is about the passing of power from an absolute monarch who owned every ounce of English soil and wielded total dominion over every human being walking upon it. Every crime was an offence against the King and punishable only by him; and as he was the sole fountain of justice, no wrong or mistake of law could find redress except through him; all our laws were his decrees; all taxation was levied by him alone and it was paid over to him personally to spend as he alone decided.

The power of taxation mattered to an absolute monarch as much as to the most democratic of governments, for without it all his other powers became a sham. Without it he was powerless to defend the country from external enemies and powerless to do good or ill internally, neither able to oppress and subjugate nor to do anything a more enlightened ruler might prefer. Revenue is the supply of ways and means of government: that very word Supply (for constitutional historians adorn it with a capital initial letter) imports the core of a dispute that went on for 900 years. It was not until 1860 that Lord Palmerston successfully moved the Resolution:

> "That the right of granting Aids and Supplies to the Crown is in the Commons alone as an essential part of their Constitution; and the limitation of all such Grants as to the matter, manner, measure and time is only in them..."
> " to secure to the Commons their rightful control over Taxation and Supply, this House has in its own hands a power so to impose and remit Taxes..."

The final stage of the transfer of that last power to the elected representatives of the people who actually paid the taxes did not come, some would say, until 1928, the year when the franchise was granted to all adults, men and women, equally. Not until then was the House of Commons representative of all adult taxpayers and thus equipped with democratic authority to tax the British people. In the intervening years wars were fought, thousands killed and many more punished in sundry ways to settle who exercised the power of taxation.

In fact, the control over taxation is more important today than centuries ago when we were ruled by an absolute monarch. Not that the scale and scope of taxation is higher today (in some ways the burden is easier now); but the more questionable the motives of those who raise the revenue, the more necessary it is to make sure that they are satisfactorily controlled. Behind the outward face of idealism, there lurks the thirst for power as the force to drive on the ambitious politician; and the climb to the top in gaining a nation's leadership can rarely, if ever, be made unless that force is strong. An absolute monarch born to succeed his father may be

45

mercifully free of that propelling thirst for power; most of our Kings, if not our Queens, were of that happier disposition. Hence something of a paradox: in our democratic system firm and clear safeguards are needed to circumscribe the power of taxation still more than was the case years ago.

In the United States this power has its special significance; ever since the Declaration of Independence the power has incontestably resided in the legislature. To this day the President must carefully and tactfully persuade Congress to vote Supply. It was Chief Justice Marshall who said "the power to tax is the power to destroy." More clearly in the United States than over here is taxation seen to be an act of confiscation, of law-abiding citizens coerced into handing over their income or their savings lawfully gained.

On January 1st 1973 this sovereign power was surrendered by our Parliament and given back to the Executive. Our import duties and levies were thenceforth fixed for us by the Council of Ministers, a supranational authority. The purpose of most of these taxes, especially those on food, is to keep out imports and so the taxes are fixed high enough to achieve that end; and as no duties or levies can be collected from this source unless the goods actually enter our ports, such revenue provides only a fraction of what the EC needs. Because these are Community taxes, their scope and rules are fixed by Community legislation.

For a single market to be established there is a strong case for other forms of taxation to be treated in the same way. For an executive, through the Council of Ministers, to take from the legislature the coercive powers of taxation is plainly a reversal of democratic principles. Yet it must be agreed that common policies will require revenue. Who is to vote Supply? At the present time the task is divided between the Council of Ministers and the

individual national legislatures. One acts supranationally and the other internationally. To allow the
Council of Ministers permanently and increasingly to
raise taxation would be such a blatant onslaught on
democratic principles that no-one is likely to urge that
course. Hence there remain two possibilities: to give the
European Parliament the power of taxation or to vest it in
the national legislatures. *There is no third way in which it can
be done.*

Next is perhaps the most signal hallmark of a nation-
state, the power to make its own laws. On this there are
sanctions to enforce obedience, otherwise a law is but a
string of empty words. But sanctions are acts of coercion,
which also have no meaning when there is no force
behind them. This power of enforcement must reside
somewhere; it must be capable of being brought into
action, readily and effectively, and if it fails, the laws
themselves will be of little value. Common policies
agreed by differing European countries may conceivably
not require their existing laws to be changed, but it is
unlikely. Pollution, company law, labour relations, social
security, exchange controls are some of the examples
that are obvious candidates for common action: each one
would need either new laws or amendment of existing
laws.

The Treaty of Rome prescribed the supranational
approach. Article 189 gives to the Council of Ministers
the power to legislate, and any law it passes comes into
effect immediately, thus by-passing the legislatures of the
member states. Article 189 sets out a procedure which
conflicts with almost every tenet of democracy. The
ministers who make the law may be elected by some kind
of constituency in their own country, but each one is a
member of his government, and both his vote and his
voice is that of the executive. Secondly, every word
spoken in the Council is secret; no reporter may attend

47

and pass on to a waiting public anything said, no more than members of the public may watch how laws are made which are to regulate their lives. Just as bad is the horse-trading which every participant confirms, for the interests of minorities in one country then get submerged to advance those of a majority elsewhere. If we are to be serious about changing the law of Europe, other means must be found. The directly elected European Parliament can be made into the body that does it, or the existing legislatures can claw back what they have lost to the Council. *There is no third way in which our laws can be made democratically.*

The last hallmark of a nation-state is about how its laws are interpreted. It is a question of jurisprudence. The Treaty of Rome makes the European Court of Justice the Supreme Court of Judicature for the United Kingdom, as it does for all the other member states. As the last Court of Appeal it interprets the law its own way and pays no regard to the principles and practice in any one member state unless they fit in with its own. For Continental Europe no problem arises, for all those ten member states have much the same principles and practice, In the United Kingdom and, largely, in Ireland, it is different. Our lawyers speak of the Golden Rule: our statutes and regulations must be interpreted strictly and the legislature is assumed by our courts to intend the ordinary meaning of the words used. The main purpose of the Golden Rule is to put everyone equal before the law because everyone must be deemed to understand the ordinary meaning of the words. But often this ordinary meaning may clash with what others might assume was the intention of the legislators. For this reason judges on the Continent often interpret a statute according to what they call "the spirit of the law" as well.

So far it might be said that the distinction does not matter very much, and if we and the Irish were to adopt

48

the Continental approach no harm would ensue. But the Golden Rule stems from our whole national attitude to law and order. Law is an absolute thing to us; we break it or we do not. It is not to be disobeyed because you yourself do not think the spirit of it is offended. The Anglo-Saxon principle (and it stretches throughout the English-speaking world) is objective; the Continental, subjective; and so long as the subjects of the realm can let their own special pleading persuade them what is the law, a disdain for its validity will grow with its volume. A Europe of common policies will offer too many opportunities for that kind of special pleading.

It means, of course, that laws should be interpreted in the same way as they are made, either supranationally or nationally. To have laws passed at Westminster interpreted in Luxembourg by the European Court of Justice will not do, any more than the contrary. *If justice is to be consistent, there is no third way.* To make the principles and practice of interpretation the same is not a concession to a supranational authority, for it can be done by national legislators by agreement with each other and put into effect by each supreme court. If changes in the law are needed, it is the way to let them come with the least amount of friction.

Anyone who dismisses these matters as niceties or pedantries fails to see that each one is about power — the power of the state over the individual. Each of the powers implies coercion and the taking away from the individual citizen the freedom he or she would otherwise enjoy. New policies for a group of European countries may sound fine in the abstract. When they come to be put into practice they may enhance our lives and better our future, but a price must still be paid for them. That price is likely to be at least two-fold: a change in our laws and an increase in taxation. Both are curbs upon freedom. Any new law puts a curb on someone's freedom to behave as he or she wishes and it may curb the freedom of the majority. Any increase of taxation puts another limit upon the citizen's freedom to spend his or her money as he or she might wish. A government can "do" nothing for us unless it takes away our freedom or our money, and usually it is both. A supranational authority is no different.

The Council of Ministers being an unelected body and primarily answerable to the national governments, no-one claims its methods of making our laws or raising taxes are democratic. Its members may report back to their national parliaments, but this makes it only indirectly accountable to an electorate. Second-hand accountability is no substitute for the real thing. It is scarcely an example for others to follow, and this must be said especially of countries in Eastern Europe as they strive for self-government; and in the erstwhile colonies of Asia and Africa there will be an uncertain future for democracy if a country like Britain is seen to shed the characteristics of parliamentary government.

Would it put matters right if the Community were to become a federal union? Later chapters suggest that the sheer bigness of such a union would create a democratic deficit even greater than exists already. It is true, however, that a federal constitution transfers fiscal, legislative and treaty-making powers to supranational institutions that are made answerable to the people, who have an influence on how they are exercised through elected representatives. The President of the United States of America is effectively elected by all the people; Congress is unequivocally so, and the Supreme Court, the last arbiter of the laws passed by Congress, has its members approved by it. When distinguished policitians claim that a federal Europe is a faraway dream or "not on the immediate agenda", as they are heard to say, they fail to understand the constitutional significance of what has happened. The Community, so long as it retains its supranational nature, must transform itself from an emerging unitary mega-state to a federal union or abandon any pretence to be run on democratic principles. In the hope that the latter is not to be the choice, it follows that the Community can travel along on one road only. Legislative, fiscal and treaty-making powers must pass to the only democratically-elected body in the Community, namely the European Parliament. The powers that it thus acquires must inevitably be taken away from the House of Commons and the other national parliaments, and also to some extent from the national governments. This will arouse opposition from most of them. The only possible alternative, if the principles of democracy are to be followed, is to change direction towards a partnership of nation-states. That, of course, requires the legislative, fiscal and treaty-making powers of the Council of Ministers to be transferred back to the national parliaments, for the European Parliament to resume a consultative status and for the European Court of Justice to lose its role as the supreme court of judicature. We deceive ourselves if we believe there can be a third road to go down.

3

Unity and Freedom; Order and Diversity

That the size of states should gradually increase has been an accepted truth for several generations; in Europe, Bismarck's Germany and Garibaldi's Italy bore witness to what many historians and economists looked upon as an inevitable trend. Just as primitive families united to form tribes which merged to become nations, so in the modern world smaller nations would unite to form mega-states and in due course these too would come together to create a single world order. Since man was, as Aristotle told us, a gregarious animal, he required a social order in which to fulfil his needs; and the more those needs expanded so the wider the society must become for their fulfilment. How to strike a balance between freedom and order, between the natural right to freedom and the need for social order, has been the battlefield for political philosophers even before Aristotle and will remain so for ever. Individual freedom begets diversity, while order ensures unity. Is there, then, a balance to be found between unity and diversity? In the context of Europe's future the question seems to be crucial. In a mega-state of over three hundred million individuals, to what extent can the single individual be free to do what he or she would wish; and what degree of unity must there be to ensure order among so many millions? The European Community of Six has expanded to Twelve without, it seems, these matters being discussed, let alone settled. Unless political philosophers have been debating an irrelevance, it is surely time for some thought to be given to where freedom ends and unity begins in a Community which has no parallel in history.

To suggest, as some have done, that the United States of America can inspire an answer is to overlook some critical differences. Over ninety percent of her people, as immigrants over the centuries, went there to salute a common flag, share the same ideals of liberty and justice, speak in one language and therefore enjoy the same culture; order and unity can come quite naturally in such circumstances. More important, constitutionally, is that each of the states was much the same in size and strength as the others; New York and California may be larger than their neighbours but a federal constitution has succeeded in preventing either of them acquiring a dominant role. The federal systems of both Canada and Australia have also shown how important it is that the component states should be of similar size and strength. In Switzerland — the Swiss Confederation, officially — infinite pains were taken to make sure the twenty-two cantons were evenly matched, with the result that none of the three racial elements — French, German or Italian — was able to gain dominion over the other two. The Federal Republic of Germany, however, is an example of some imbalance and there are strains to show for it. Then there is the Soviet Union: Russia is manifestly the dominant state, and one by one the lesser states in the union are becoming not a little fractious. The failure to have each individual state of more or less equal size and strength led to the collapse of the Central African Federation and the West Indian Federation. The world and its history books are searched in vain for a successful precedent for a federal union without this balance between member states. Hence the interest shown by some European federalists in the maps of 18th century Europe. To make a federal union work, they acknowledge, the United Kingdom must be dissolved so that it will be England, Wales, Scotland and Northern Ireland that would be the member states of the union; in the same way, France, Spain, Italy and Western Germany would have their bio-regions restored, and Belgium would be divided without difficulty into two natural regions.

The accepted truth that man must live in ever enlarging social orders seems, however, to have been in recent years rather less of a certitude. Among the 159 countries in the United Nations, none outside Europe is clamouring very loudly to abandon its status as a nation-state. Some of them are very small and too small to be "viable" in the opinion of an earlier generation of economists. Viable, means, so the dictionary says, capable of sustaining life. In some of them life seems remarkably congenial. If Liechtenstein with a population of 28,000 is not the smallest nation state in the world, it is incontestably the one with the highest standard of living. That the explanation lies in the number of trusts and financial corporations that have made it a tax haven is not good enough: these financial interests went to Liechtenstein because it was already a tax haven. Taxes were negligible long before any of them arrived for the good reason that the government itself was negligible. No-one describes the attractions of Liechtenstein more engagingly than Leopold Kohr: in that country, he says, anyone can telephone the Prince and you get through immediately to

55

hear his voice answer, "This is the government speaking." In fact, the trusts and other financial concerns, having descended upon the little country, have done little to benefit its people; by bringing in most of their own staff, they have caused the population to double in size, which in turn has made great demands upon housing, hospitals and the transport system, and it is doubtful whether the indigenous Liechtensteiners have gained any net benefit in return.

Although Liechtenstein is scarcely a paradigm for a country such as Britain with a population two thousand times larger, she shows how extreme smallness and extreme prosperity can blend together. More persuasive, perhaps, is any handbook on European economic statistics. Whatever yardstick one takes to measure prosperity, the smaller countries of Western Europe enjoy higher standards than their immediate and larger neighbours. Were the Nordic countries of Iceland, Norway, Sweden and Finland to unite into one, would their prosperity rise? As it is, the standard of living and the quality of life are demonstrably better than those prevailing throughout almost all parts of the European Community. In none of those four countries does one find the evils of long term unemployment, slum areas, industrial decay or other symptoms of chronic poverty; the excessively rich are few and the excessively poor invisible; and every town is witness to a sense of general well-being. It is, indeed, fertile ground for unity. Then travel through the towns of Britain, Germany and Italy; despite a few notable exceptions, one soon comes face to face with all those perceptible signs that point to areas of poverty and decay. Equally, this is far from being fertile ground for social unity, without which resentment, despair and alienation — the symptoms of social division — are there instead. Nor is it just in cities the size of Liverpool, Birmingham, Lyon, Marseilles, Milan, Frankfurt and Hamburg that this evidence of disunity can be perceived; it is apparent, too, in the smaller towns comparable in size to those of the Nordic countries.

When Bismarck created the German Reich, he did so on the pretext, so he claimed, that if all Germans united together, a greater degree of prosperity would ensue. The Germans of Austria and Switzerland stayed beyond his embrace, yet their economic well-being has been no less than their fellow Germans who responded to his call to unity. That Austrians and German-Swiss seem to have the same sense of social unity as is to be seen in the countries of Scandinavia confirms the tendency that the people in smaller countries are spared the divisiveness that follows from extremes of wealth. Among Austrians and German-Swiss one finds no areas of poverty as one does in Germany itself. Why is this so? Whichever of those three countries he is in, he is still a German of, one would imagine, much the same instincts, temperament, culture and other influences. Whatever the reason, it is difficult to believe that the smallness of Austria and Switzerland has deprived the Germans living there of any economic or social advantage. All the evidence suggests that a small country, hence a small domestic market, is no less economically "viable" than a large country; and in a small country the extreme poverty is avoided, with a greater sense of social unity thus prevailing.

All the smaller countries of the developed world are characterised by a degree of social homogeneity which is seldom found in the larger countries. With this homogeneity there is no place for an alienated minority; social unity is the consequence; and hence no submerged underclass, neither a legion of dropouts nor a high level of crime, all three of which now blight every large country in the developed world.

Both Leopold Kohr in the *Breakdown of Nations* and Fritz Schumacher in *Small is Beautiful* showed how small

57

countries had an advantage over their larger neighbours. Everything that has to be organised requires a structure and, therefore, a size. To achieve their goal, some need to be big, others small; what is important is to discover the appropriate size of the structure. As the structure of a country is fixed by its frontiers, its citizens will, generally speaking, live their lives within their national frontiers. The larger the structure of a country, the more its people are tempted to become footloose, tempted to move into its larger towns in search of fortune or excitement or to escape failure or disgrace. Thus the larger town becomes a great city; and as the footloose are just as likely to fail in their quest as to succeed, the areas of poverty grow and social cohesion breaks down.

Bismarck also failed to annex Denmark. What would have happened to the Danes had he succeeded? As with Austria and German Switzerland, the level of prosperity in Denmark has been, on the whole, higher than in Germany; but the Danes are not Germans. Once absorbed into the Reich they would have become a racial minority, Copenhagen a provincial city and Danish a secondary language. Germany herself would not be a circle of integrated common interests, without which national unity is a charade. Bismarck would have stood upon a Reich greater in size but lacking homogeneity, the essential ingredient of unity, and his Reich would have been intrinsically weakened. Germany would have lost its homogeneity and the Danes would have exchanged the freedom to govern themselves for a kind of unity.

Does this suggest that freedom (and the consequent diversity) and order (and the consequent unity) are in conflict? In matters of decision-making we have a need for both freedom and unity. There is a sphere of human activity where freedom is appropriate; and another sphere where there ought to be unity. The problem arises in identifying the two spheres, and fixing their territory.

Bismarck's view of the sphere of freedom and unity for the people of Denmark would have been distinctly diferent from that of a contemporary and perceptive Danish citizen. Every terrorist leader in the last half-century has shouted loudly for freedom; when it is come, he has changed the tune to unity. Dictators the world over have every reason to call for unity. But in the democracies, too, one never can be quite certain what some politicians mean when they speak of either freedom or unity. On their lips the two spheres are the victims of obfuscation. For as long as politics answers the question, "Who does what to whom?" the governors will look at freedom and unity through a different window from the governed. Let ordinary people beware; let them look more carefully when it comes to decision-making, at what they, rather than the politicians, need by way of freedom and unity.

Let us take first the appropriate sphere for freedom. Whatever our material needs may be, we gain the most benefit when we are able to enjoy the widest choice. The most important of them all, the freedom to buy any kind of food from any part of the world is one which gives the opportunity to buy at the lowest price as well as to choose whatever one feels like eating; and any diminution of that freedom is a diminution of one, if not both, of those advantages. A policy of self-sufficiency in food, as in most things, tends to be self-defeating, even self-contradictory. How can one tell the people of any country, no matter how well it may be endowed with the gifts of nature, that they shall eat the produce of their native soil and none other, without putting a limit upon their freedom of choice? They may know nothing of some delicacy grown in some far away land; ignorance of what they are missing is no substitute for the freedom, trivial though it may be, that they have lost. The same principle of free trade applies to any one of our material wants. The

59

most satisfied motorist must be the one who has had the freedom to try out all the cars in the world and whose government has allowed him to buy the one of his choice without artifically raising its price by putting a tariff upon it. In satisfying any of our material needs, it is difficult to think of any limit upon our freedom which is in our interests.

As man does not live by bread alone, let us turn to our intellectual and spiritual needs. Again, to open up to us all the art, philosophy, music, literature and religions that the world can offer is to allow us the freedom to decide what is the most appropriate choice. In this, as in fulfilling our material needs, we cannot have too much freedom and if good things are to be found on Mars, not even the freedom of our own planet is enough.

The third category of the global dimension is the protection of the environment. Nations ought to be at liberty to agree with others, no matter where on the globe, to safeguard many matters, the sum total of which we call our environment. For a nation to have a fetter placed upon its freedom to make treaties with others, as the Treaty of Rome does, is to put a limit upon what Britain or any other member state of the European Community can do in reaching an agreement outside Europe to promote the environment.

The other sphere where unity takes its place concerns our relations with other people. The fewer people we have to relate to, the easier it is. The more employees in a company the more time is spent by the management in explaining what has to be done, and the greater is the risk of strikes and disruption; the more pupils in a class, the more teachers' skills are tested; the larger the army, the more careful its commander must be in sending down the orders for battle; and many a committee chairman wishes he sat alone. Athough many a big organisation can work harmoniously and many a small one have its dissensions, nonetheless the business of human relations inevitably becomes more difficult as the size of a unit gets bigger. The reason is simple enough: unity, defined, is the quality of a unit, and unity is amazingly easy to achieve when the unit is one person. Napoleon, as his troops strode out of France, no more wanted them to believe themselves free to fight how and when they liked than Henry Ford wished his employees to think themselves free to make his cars just as they pleased.

So the spheres of unity and freedom are distinct. How are they, then, allocated in a mega-state embracing over 300 million people? The large market which it constitutes for food and other material wants, large though it is, remains puny compared with what the world can offer: to take away the liberty of 300 million people to buy the food that they might prefer, because it happens to be purchased outside the Community, whether by tariffs or outright prohibition, is manifestly a curb upon a legitimate freedom.

Although we can assume there will be freedom to satisfy the spiritual, intellectual and artistic needs, there is one freedom which would lose its potency, namely the freedom of speech. True, no fetter would be placed upon it explicitly, but if its purpose is to change the opinion of others, the smaller the number of people one seeks to persuade, the more potent is this most precious of freedoms. To persuade one's neighbours in a village is work for a simple tongue; to convince a county demands much more; and so much more again to sway a whole nation. One man's voice, even in Churchillian cadences, is lost among 300 million people. In a modern society a long list of pressure groups, charities and other good causes must influence the government to achieve a purpose — the RSPCA, Age Concern, Friends of the Earth, and Consumer Watch are examples. The promotion of animal welfare, consumer protection, medical research

61

and care of the countryside have become matters of government responsibility, and a number of civil servants spend their whole time on each of these subjects. Matching them may be two or more outside bodies, funded mainly by voluntary contributions from the public, and a large part of their work consists in feeding civil servants with information and ideas. It may be said that these many pressure groups are themselves a product of large-scale government, for in a small state, where communication between government and governed is simple, there is little necessity for people to raise a collective voice to enable themselves to be heard. The larger the unit of government and the larger the number of governed, the more the need for pressure groups arises and the more resources they must have to do their job. Whether the existence of these pressure groups in the place of an individual's voice serves to advance democracy may be a little questionable.

These pressure groups have their counterparts in the form of industrial and commercial interests; and in several fields they see themselves as adversaries. The pesticide manufacturers joust with Friends of the Earth; the food industry with Consumer Watch, and the drug companies with the National Anti-Vivisection Society. The lobbying and counter-lobbying that ensues is sometimes described as part of the modern democratic process. To call it a necessary by-product of a large state might be rather more accurate. Democracy, after all, is about people; and if democracy declares that we are all civically equal, a government which finds itself so extended that it cannot govern without paying heed to citizens banded in pressure groups on the one hand and the collective voice of numerous large companies on the other is taking a step which seems to deny the principle of civic equality.

The smaller the state the more the ordinary citizen can

be heard; and, what is just as important, the more he or she will feel his or her voice will have some effect. How often do we hear someone say, "*they* won't listen". A sense of impotence and a feeling that one's own efforts will be futile are endemic in a large state. To get the Town Hall crowded, call a meeting to discuss whether the new by-pass should go east or west; the public feel that their attendance will have some effect. But hold a meeting about a great national issue and just a handful may abandon the television or the garden. Is it that people are not interested, or that in their opinion it will make no difference to what happens whether they attend or not?

Unity in a tiny state comes naturally. The fewer the inhabitants, the fewer the conflicting interests that will arise, and the consequent harmony enables laws to be made which cause no injustice. Minorities there may be and they may be weak and inarticulate, but in a small state, given freedom of speech, they will be heard. Small is indeed democratic. Mega-states, it may be said, are not made by God for the good of ordinary people; they are the artefacts of politicians who thirst for power. Mega-states may serve the purpose of great international companies, but not ordinary people. A deeper Europe as it moves towards a unitary mega-state would be in danger of putting unity in the sphere where freedom belongs and freedom in the sphere where unity belongs. A wider Europe, however, is capable of putting these two where, for ordinary people, they both should be.

4

Small Is Economic, Too

Small is democratic. At least, those who entice us along the road to a huge supranational union should be made to prove that the concentration of power a superstate gathers to its capital city will not leave ordinary people — the nine hundred and ninety nine out of a thousand, let us say — with a feeling of powerlessness over how their lives are governed. A rising tide of prosperity affording the millions a steadily higher standard of living will amply compensate for that, so the rejoinder goes, because a larger and more dynamic economy will provide tangible benefits to set against intangible feelings. The supranationalists in the 1960s and 1970s, when discussing how to coax the public to go their way, would say quite frankly that the people of Western Europe, once seeing those tangible benefits, would acquiesce in the transfer of power from their nation-states to supranational institutions. Yet does it follow that a much enlarged economy will necessarily generate the additional wealth? Countries in Western Europe which remain outside the EC are not markedly poorer than those inside. As was pointed out in the previous chapter, a glance at Switzerland, Norway and Sweden gives us a picture of economic stability, no serious unemployment, and a general sense of well-being in all parts of each of those countries. There are few depressed areas comparable to our own and little call for regional aid. Indeed, nothing seems to be wrong with any of their economies: they jog along without headlines about crises and crashes. As members of the European Free Trade Association their exports have tariff-free access to the EC, but that is not an obvious advantage, as the principle of reciprocity requires them to give similar access to imports from the EC. Now, if it be true that a large integrated economy has an advantage over a small one, we would expect to have seen damage to Norway, Sweden, and Switzerland. Of that there is not the slightest evidence: and any study of those three small-scale economies shows that the opposite seems to be the case. Who can deny they are three prosperous countries with contented people? Are we deafened by cries of anguish as their people lose their jobs and go hungry? Do we see their Prime Ministers trailing to Brussels to beg admission to the rich man's club?

Norway came near to joining the EC at the same time as the UK. Together with Denmark and the Republic of Ireland, negotiations took place and the terms of entry were agreed, subject to a referendum. The people of Norway were assured by politicians and industrialists that disaster would befall them were they to be such "little Norwegians" as to vote "No"; their industries would be cut off and unable to compete, unemployment and poverty would follow, and — the ultimate threat — should the Norwegians show themselves up as being bad Europeans by voting against entry on the generous terms they had been offered, then "Europe" would not treat them kindly in the future when they were subsequently forced to reapply for membership. The arguments deployed, therefore, were much the same as in the United Kingdom. Despite the vast sums of money the industrialists spent on the campaign, the people of Norway rejected membership by a small majority. Not one of the threats materialised; Norway's prosperity has steadily risen, and any Norwegian who might murmur that their decision was a mistake would now be considered a little eccentric. True, Norway has her share of North Sea oil, but so has the UK. The difference is that Norway is husbanding her reserves for the twenty-first century, while the UK is selling oil at a rate which some observers consider to be extremely unwise. What we are doing is to sell much of this oil to the rest of the Community on terms unfavourable to ourselves, lest a Community energy policy should be imposed. We have been reminded by our partners that just as the fish swimming in that part of the North Sea which once used to be British waters now belong to the Community, so the oil under the fish also belongs, and for the same reason. Norway, by staying outside the Community, has exclusive rights over Norwegian waters, and so can decide for herself what should be done with her own oil.

Everything, as Kohr and Schumacher have shown, has its appropriate size. An entire industry or a separate business concern within it has an optimum scale of operation: it must strive to match the potential demand from the public for its services or products with its own supply. Assessing potential demand may be difficult for any businessman: and the directors in control of a very large company, attempting to meet what they believe will be the demand, may organise the production of millions of their product rather than thousands or hundreds. The larger the demand their business is trying to satisfy, the more difficult it is to judge with precision. The proprietor of a village shop knows that three hundred people live in the vicinity and nearly all of them like to eat oranges; and if one week he miscalculates how many they will want to buy, he may lose a little money, but his miscalculation will scarcely have a devastating effect upon the nation's economy. A businessman trying to please hundreds of customers is less likely to make a mistake with serious consequences than one trying to please thousands, still less than the businessman who sets out to please millions.

A typical depressed town is to be found where two or three very large businesses have been the backbone of the local economy and, having established their dominant position in the area, later miscalculate the future demand for what they are supplying. A thousand firms all employing ten people pose less of a risk to an area than ten firms each with a thousand on its payroll. Depressed areas crying out for regional aid are not a feature of the small state: in large integrated markets they seem to be endemic.

Large-scale businesses with thousands in their workshops and millions in their cashflows may be indispensable in a modern society. However, that does not detract from the essential point that the small-scale business, being easier to manage, is less likely to make serious mistakes with rippling effects throughout the whole of a nation's economy. Recognising the necessity for large-scale businesses ought not to blind us to the potential damage they can do.

Perhaps the company capable of causing the most damage of all is the one which has acquired a dominant position in a large market. Sloth (that dreadful sin which in this context means an indifference towards the consumer's welfare) sets in. Why innovate, if the product still sells? Why worry too much about maintaining good industrial relations when a monopoly or near-monopoly makes you impervious to the consequences of restrictive practices? And why worry about wage demands when the extra cost can be passed on to the customer? The British shipbuilding industry once had such a dominant position in the largest market of all, that of the world; and therein lay the seeds of its own decay and demise. Much the same can be said for other parts of British manufacturing industry that once swept all before them, but have since sunk to obscurity. A large protected market, such as the single market of the EC, has this great danger: it can give large companies the opportunity to grow very large indeed; and once they have achieved a dominant place in the protected market, a decline sets in, and the jobs of thousands are in jeopardy and whole areas may be blighted by a depression.

Once the comfort of a safe internal market begets the sin of sloth, as it always seems to do, dissatisfied customers will eventually turn to some kind of alternative. A new competitor within the market may rise up, the foreign competitor succeed despite the barriers or an alternative kind of product may take possession. Whichever of the three follows, the decline of the great multinational company will almost certainly bring misfortune, even disaster, to thousands of people. It is difficult to imagine a multiplicity of small companies having that effect, for the competition between them will give the customers enough choice to prevent indifference to their welfare.

Neither the small company nor the customer has much to gain from a large-scale integrated market. The latter implies a customs union; and as is seen in a later chapter, the customer gains most in conditions of free trade, when the freedom of choice is maximised; and in the absence of an open world economy with total free trade, the next best thing for the customer is a free trade area, which is essentially different from a customs union

69

such as the EC.

As to the small company — any company, let us say, that is plainly not a multinational — if it is capable of satisfying its customers in conditions of free competition, it has nothing to fear from a policy of free trade. It has, however, two reasons for being apprehensive of a customs union which extends over numerous countries to form a large single market. A customs union is by definition protectionist: there are tariffs and non-tariff barriers, and there is also a central regulation of the internal market. Who does this regulating? It is not a national government — supervised by a national parliament with a member representing the area where the company is based. The regulation of the market is done supranationally; and in the case of the EC it is done in Brussels by the Commission proposing regulations which the Council of Ministers adopt, modify or reject. These regulations are all-important: they are the law which governs how companies act. Why, we might ask ourselves, do all the major multinational companies have offices in Brussels? They act as listening posts and the headquarters for lobbying; their staff get to know the officials of the Commission, and the latter freely acknowledge that in reaching their decisions they consult the representatives of these companies. The regulation of the market by the Commission is done to protect the market and although the Commission tries to do much to protect the consumer, when it comes to the interests of the producer, it is not unreasonable to assume that those interests which are articulated across the table by the local lobby are more likely to be heard and acted upon than the interests of the smaller companies whose managers are far away in Glasgow, perhaps, or Lisbon or Copenhagen, unaware of what is going on.

The other reason for their apprehension is that any business requires a market of the appropriate size for the scale of its production. The demand for Rolls-Royces is very small: that obviously does not imply that Rolls-Royce needs a market of only a single English county, for the more expensive and luxurious the item made, the wider the market desirable. Nothing less than the whole world suits Rolls-Royce. So, too, with some of the Swiss watch manufacturers. They may be very small businesses, employing perhaps four or five skilled craftsmen, and no-one hears them calling for a large single market because they succeed in selling watches to rich people in any country in the world. The vast majority of small companies, providing goods or services less exciting than a Rolls-Royce or a gold timepiece, want a market of corresponding modesty. Like the village garage which satisfies a few hundred local motorists, the small business does best when close to its customers; their needs are better understood, their complaints quickly remedied, costs of transport are less and everything else that accompanies a good service is more satisfactory. And if it is not, then another small business will soon move in. A single market of 300 million people is, almost invariably, either too big or too small for efficient businesses which do not need any kind of protection. The small company which supplies the kind of things which we all buy will flourish among a few million people at most; and the company specialising in some luxury item prospers when able to sell to rich people wherever they are.

Leopold Kohr in his excellent book, the *Breakdown of Nations*, wrote of economies outgrowing their strength. We see the signs of this when they incur costs which small economies succeed in avoiding. Professor Kohr put these costs under three headings. First came what he called power commodities. Assuming the economy is to some degree regulated, as it must be in a customs union, the larger it grows the more costly is any effective administration. Power moves to the centre and the further away the centre is from the periphery, the more difficult and complicated the task of monitoring the effects of the controls and regulations and assessing any change that may be needed.

The second cost arises out of what Professor Kohr described as density commodities. A large integrated market will create a number of areas where growth will be greater than elsewhere, usually in city conurbations where several million people will come to live. This, of course, happened in the United Kingdom which in Professor Kohr's terms had, even before entering the EEC, an economy which was overgrown. The metropolitan areas of London, Birmingham, Merseyside, Glasgow and, perhaps, even Tyneside, became so densely populated that all sorts of costs were imposed upon the economy which would not have arisen if they had remained half or a quarter of their size. An underground railway system has to be built to get a large proportion of the people to work: even so, those who travel above ground by car or bus find their journey takes twice as long as it would in a market town, so new roads must be built, one-way systems introduced, innumerable traffic lights installed and so forth. The concrete jungle of the conurbation may or may not contribute to crime, but the amount of crimes committed, of all kinds, in relation to the population, always seems to be greater in these areas of overgrowth; and the subsequent cost must take into account not only the quantifiable expense of higher insurance premiums, additional police, court trials and prison sentences, but also the unquantifiable cost of human misery.

The third cost is that of progress commodities. Vast six-lane motorways are not seen across Liechtenstein; they are not even found in Norway or Sweden, two countries as prosperous as any. The bigger the integrated market, the more goods must travel the length and breadth of it, so a criss-cross of roads is needed, but never is it said that the roads system is adequate. The demand for ever more road improvements goes on, unabated even by the most ambitious of programmes of road-works. This progress affords us a higher standard of living, so we are told, but as we queue to get on to the motorways, or as nearby residents sniff the diesel fumes, such progress may be seen as something of a chimera. The standard of living is as much about qualities as quantities, and the quality of life tends to decline in a vast integrated economy, except for the richer sections of society who can afford, for example, a chauffeur-driven limousine instead of the over-crowded bus.

These three groups of costs which have to be borne by a large-scale economy, but not a small one, magnify the damage done whenever there is a downturn in consumer demand. A small economy can quickly adapt to a modest recession and, because producer and consumer are more closely linked, the effect of a recession is detected more quickly and remedial action can be taken. In the large integrated market, these danger signals take longer to get through; and when the recession comes the three groups of costs that Professor Kohr lists still have to be borne. The smaller economy, being spared them, is able to get through the recession more easily. This is why trade cycles have greater consequences in the United States than in a smaller country just as industrialised such as, say, Sweden. Nor is the danger confined to the capitalist world. The Soviet Union has fared just as badly and in some respects worse, as Professor Kohr has recorded. The reason why very large companies, whether or not multinational, are so anxious to seek from governments some form of protectionism is that they tend to be inherently inefficient. Professor Kohr, who made a special study of them, attributed this failure to the law of diminishing productivity. He defines the latter in this way:

If we add variable units of any factor of production to a fixed quantity of another, a point will be reached beyond which each additional unit of the variable factor adds less to the total product than the preceding one.

Each of the four factors of production (land, labour, capital and enterprise) may be fixed; and, generally speaking, enterprise or the entrepreneurial capacity of the managers is always so. Now if one or more of the other three factors is increased, a rise in productivity will be likely to follow. This may tempt management to add a further increase of that factor, but this time the rise in productivity would not be quite so great as it was previously; and less great again if a third increase is made. Let us imagine any factory: it has a given size on a particular piece of ground, a workforce of a certain strength, capital of a specified amount and a management of some ability, though that is less definable than the other three elements. The management decides to employ another man on the shop floor to speed up the work. That result achieved, it is decided a second man would speed up production still more. Whatever advantage gained by engaging a second man, it will be not quite so good as the result of what the first was able to achieve.

Looking again at the four factors of production, we see that each of the quantifiable ones can be increased without much difficulty. The fourth factor, management, is not a matter of quantity but of quality. To increase the quality of management is always feasible, for it can be done by recruiting a new team or by sending the existing team away to learn how to do their job better or by themselves deciding to manage differently. This has been the case in most large companies in recent decades. No major company, it may be said, is managed on the same principles as it was by an earlier generation, for the techniques of management have become sophisticated

74

and scientific. Above all, the very large companies now tend to delegate considerably and operate through semi-autonomous subsidiaries. True though this is, the heads of large companies will admit that they remain responsible for the major decisions relating to their company's enterprise. It means, of course, that the enterprise factor remains largely, if not totally, static.

The law of diminishing productivity is, therefore, unflattering to big business concerns. They can increase the number of factories, the size of their workforce and the amount of capital invested, but the more they do, the less productive are those increases. Managerial talent has its limitations and, because there is an optimum size for the ability of any manager, once that size is exceeded, so the manager is less able to manage it successfully. Everyone has a story to tell about a big company making a mistake over an order or providing an unsatisfactory service, which would not have happened had it been a one-man business. Assuming someone running a one-man business can understand what he says to himself, such a concern is quite extraordinarily easy to manage. Once he takes on an assistant, there is something of a quantum leap needed in his gifts of management, but after a while he learns how to manage his workforce of one. But he may find it extraordinarily difficult when he comes to handling a thousand employees. And his customers will find they don't get anything like such good service as when the whole of the firm was just the other side of the counter. When giant industrial companies call for a multinational economy with 300 million people because only such a market can enable them to reach their potential in profitability, and, moreover, they give considerable sums of money to political organisations to promote the idea of such a huge market, the rest of us might remember the law of diminishing productivity. If a large single market gives an advantage to large

75

companies over smaller ones, it is to the detriment of efficiency and the welfare of the general public.

Markets, like business units themselves, have an optimum size. When it comes to the political and legal control over a market, there is something comparable to the law of diminishing productivity. A market which is run totally on *laissez-faire* principles self-evidently requires less management. It is, in fact, self-managing with everyone who makes any kind of business decision able to do what he likes without reference to some authority; and so no wise people are employed in the task of trying to control it. A few laws passed to regulate how the market is to work will introduce the need for a proportionately modest amount of wisdom in those who make and enforce the laws. The more the market becomes planned, the greater the degree of wisdom — and the other qualities — required.

When the process of central control goes so far as the system which has hitherto existed in the Soviet Union, human talent is not to be found equal to the task. In the case of an integrated market in Europe, we ought to ask ourselves to what extent we want it to be planned, controlled and regulated. To satisfy the wants of 300 million people is daunting work; to delegate it to millions of individual businesses to do it simply in accordance with the laws of supply and demand would be an excellent idea to some people, but in the modern climate of opinion unlikely for many years to come. The more it is desired to regulate an economy, the greater the need for smallness. No doubt, a dozen shipwrecked sailors may run a communist economy on their island without too much inefficiency or too many injustices. Few people wishing most of Western Europe to be an integrated economy in one large circle will also wish it to be run on communist lines. But the EC Commission is interventionist or it is nothing. When an authority intervenes between a buyer and a seller, in the name of protecting one or the other or society generally, it cannot always take into account the eccentric whims and wishes of everyone subject to its decree. Dissatisfaction and loss of economic welfare naturally follow, but both are much reduced when government and governed are close together, just as the customer tends to get more satisfaction from the one-man business.

5

Customs Union or Free Trade Area

Whether a wider Europe is based on a customs union or
free trade area, far from being an arcane question, goes
to the very root of the issue. It is important constitutionally, even ecologically, as well as economically;
and it has immense consequences for the future development of world trade, especially for the Third World.
There are powerful reasons why a wider Europe will fail
as a customs union, yet the Treaty of Rome is quite
specific on the point. Article 9 states: "The Community
shall be based upon a customs union which shall cover
all trade in goods..."

As some commentators persist in speaking of the
Community as "no longer just a free trade area", let us
first be quite clear about the difference between these
two trading arrangements. Both eliminate tariffs between
the member countries and endeavour to remove the
non-tariff barriers that exist; but while in a free trade area
a member country is at liberty to trade as it wishes with
outside countries, in a customs union there must be a

common external tariff and all other barriers must be brought into line. A customs union presupposes a common commercial policy and in the case of the Community it is settled supranationally in accordance with the principle of Community Preference.

In terms of industrial trade the Community has tended to pursue a liberal policy: its average tariff on industrial goods, for example, was significantly less than what the U.K. imposed before she joined. In agricultural trade, it was the converse, the British people enjoying the advantages of virtual free trade in food. It was for this reason that General de Gaulle imposed his veto on Britain's entry to the EEC. His view was this: were Britain to lower her barriers protecting her manufacturing industries while at the same time breaking her ties with Commonwealth countries, especially Australia and New Zealand, long established sources of cheap food, the discontented new member would soon become fractious.

M. Pompidou, President of France at the time of Britain's later application to join the EEC, inherited de Gaulle's fear. He expressed his views in a television broadcast to the French people. What he said is repeated here for its historical importance in explaining why France ended her opposition to Britain's entry and also because it highlights the difference between a customs union and a free trade area as the economic foundation for the European Community's expansion.

It may be remembered that until June 1971 there were considerable doubts whether Britain's application would succeed. Negotiations had been proceeding for a year, and many well-informed commentators believed they were unlikely to succeed. Among the contentious issues unresolved were whether the developing countries of the Commonwealth, such as Barbados and Mauritius, would be allowed to export sugar to the UK when the

Common Market was already self-sufficient, and whether New Zealand butter and lamb could be imported; there was also the problem of our contribution to the Community's budget and the future of sterling as a reserve currency; also our territorial rights of fishing in what were still exclusively British waters. In the dining room and smoking room of the House of Commons where MPs have discussions among themselves, often more illuminating than what they say publicly in the Chamber, almost every voice was pessimistic about an agreement being reached. The obstacles were intractable; and even Geoffrey Rippon, the Minister in charge of the negotiations, on his return from his forays to the capitals across the Channel was unable to dispel the fears of another veto.

Then, on June 20th, Mr. Heath went to Paris to spend a weekend with the French President. On his return, the Prime Minister made a statement in the House about the discussions that had taken place, but nothing of much significance was to be inferred. Yet from that moment, the negotiations were accelerated, the pessimism dispelled and Geoffrey Rippon strode through the lobbies of Westminster with a confident air. Within weeks the terms of our entry were settled. What had been said between Mr. Heath and M. Pompidou to effect this remarkable change in the climate?

On June 24th, M. Pompidou went before the television cameras to give the French people his account of the meeting. The transcript was translated into English and copies sent to the French Embassy in London. Only a limited few seem to have been distributed. This is the core of the French President's historic statement taken from that translation:

> "When I arrived in Office, Europe was in fact in deadlock. Our partners in the Europe of the Six could no longer accept that Great Britain be left out. Nor could Britain

accept any longer the Europe of the Six, which in a way reminded her of the Napoleonic Empire and the Continental blockade. General de Gaulle had in fact realised this for a long time. As early as 1958 he said to me: 'What troubles me about the Common Market is that it will make us fall out with Britain.' And, as you know, in 1968 or 1969 during the last months of his Presidency he took a step towards Great Britain which failed because of the British Government of that time.

Furthermore, I found that our partners no longer wished to progress, that the chances in particular of obtaining the renewal, and, if I may say so, the definite establishment of the Agricultural Market were very slight. That was why at the Conference of The Hague I very clearly put the bargain to them. And I obtained, on the one hand, that the Agricultural Market should become permanent in exchange, on the other hand, for the opening of negotiations with Great Britain.

Once the negotiation was open, because I do not believe in basing foreign policy on lies and hypocrisy, I considered that we had to be loyal in this negotiation and, therefore, to avoid setting traps or finding roundabout ways of barring Britain's road, that on the contrary, we had to put our questions frankly. And that was exactly what happened at, obviously, the most important moment when I had my long talk with the British Prime Minister [the few days previously].

So I put the questions in the clearest possible way. First, I said: You accept the thing which lies at the very root of the Common Market, namely Community Preference, whereby Members obtain their supplies in the first place from the Community? And the British Prime Minister confirmed in the clearest possible terms what had, in fact, already been said publicly by the British representation in Brussels.

Second question: on the functioning of the institutions and the unanimity rule to which, as you know, France is essentially attached, which means that, when a country considers that a Question is at issue, others may not impose on it the will of the majority, unanimous agreement must be reached, the British Government answered, yes, and in fact confirmed its answer publicly.

Third, the monetary question: Sterling has at present a special status, known as that of a reserve currency. It would be too complicated to explain it here, but it means that it has privileges. Obviously, in a community each member must be on an equal footing, and, therefore, the British currency must be like the others. I obtained from the British Prime Minister an undertaking that this was indeed his concept of things and that gradually — there is no question of creating a monetary crisis in the Sterling area — the Pound would become a currency like the others and would therefore participate in what we are trying to achieve: the creation of a European monetary union.

Fourth question, which was probably the most important of all: I asked the British Prime Minister what he thought of Europe, in other words, whether Britain was really determined to become European, whether Britain, which is an island, was determined to tie herself to the Continent, and whether she was prepared consequently to loosen her ties with the ocean towards which she has always looked. And I can say that the explanations and views expressed to me by Mr. Heath are in keeping with France's concept of the future of Europe and, incidentally, in keeping with what Mr. Heath has been publicly saying for twenty years."

Some years later, Mr. Roland Moyle, then MP for East Lewisham and chairman of the executive committee of the Open Seas Forum, wrote to Mr. Heath to ask him whether he agreed with M. Pompidou's account. Mr. Heath replied that talks between heads of state are held in confidence. The importance of that meeting in the context of a wider Europe is this: if Britain's entry was conditional upon the EEC remaining forever a customs union, it is difficult to see how a wider Community can espouse the principles of free trade.

The advantage of a customs union, it is often said, is

that it has more "clout" when it comes to reaching trade agreements with third countries; its voice is louder at GATT conferences, and it can stand up to protectionist threats from major industrial powers such as Japan and the United States. There is, though, a weakness in the argument. For twelve countries to speak in unison with a single voice rather than individually may well be in their interests — but only if their interests converge. The case of New Zealand illustrates this quite well. With a climate almost perfect for dairy farming, New Zealand can export butter and cheese at nearly half the price the European farmer requires; a modest limit on those exports was negotiated by the UK some years before entering the Common Market; once in, the protectionist clout against New Zealand became all-powerful and as the other member countries had no interest in importing New Zealand butter and cheese, indeed wished it to be excluded altogether, the British consumers have been required to eat much less of the butter and cheese they would prefer to buy at much lower prices.

The other argument for a customs union is constitutional; whether the Community evolves into a federal union or a unitary mega-state, it cannot avoid being a customs union. Unless the thirteen erstwhile American colonies had formed a customs union, with each state having the same tariffs and other protectionist barriers as the other twelve, settled supranationally, the Union could never have been born. So, too, with the European Community; while groups of other countries were forming free trade areas, the representatives of the Six, at the Messina Conference, quite deliberately inserted Article 9 in the Treaty of Rome as a stepping stone to what they envisaged would be a federal union.

But can a wider Europe emulate the United States of America? Can thirty-five in one Continent do what fifty have done in another? The example of Canada may show otherwise. Canada and the United States having formed a single free trade area, all tariffs and duties are being abolished throughout North America. Had Canada agreed to a customs union, her control of commercial policy would have passed to some supranational body, and as the smaller of the two, it would be in Washington rather than Ottawa that Canada's commercial policy would be settled. She would have "pooled her sovereignty" but the gain of sharing the clout of the world's most powerful economic *bloc* would have to be set against the powerlessness to safeguard her own interests when they differed from those of her partner.

In attempting to create a wider Europe we might well find Eastern European countries *vis à vis* the existing Twelve in a similar position to Canada's in relation to the United States. Canada's membership of the Commonwealth still gives her an edge in her trading links with the UK which are not loosened by joining the US in a free trade area. Countries of Eastern Europe as members of Comecon have had a relationship with the Soviet Union not too dissimilar from that which existed between Canada and the UK in the days of the Commonwealth Preference Area. So for Hungary or Poland, two obvious candidates for a wider Europe, to enter the European Community, they would have to sever their links developed through Comecon with the Soviet Union, unless the European Community became a free trade area.

The problem will not arise if Comecon is dissolved, but as its membership now extends to socialist countries outside Europe this seems unlikely; besides it would cause much loss of face in the Kremlin. Another possibility is that as the countries of Eastern Europe join the wider Europe they would leave Comecon, despite the advantages it has afforded its members. Founded in

85

1949, the Council for Mutual Economic Assistance (CMEA), as Comecon is officially called, has lived up to its name for most of its members. Originally it consisted of Albania, Bulgaria, Czechoslovakia, Hungary, Poland, Romania and the Soviet Union. Albania has left *de facto*, but over the years East Germany, Outer Mongolia, Cuba, Vietnam, North Korea, Laos, Angola and Afghanistan, Mexico, Finland and Yugoslavia have either joined or been party to its agreements. For a socialist country there are benefits in the exchange of ideas in formulating policy; of more obvious advantage is the International Bank of Economic Co-operation in the multilateral settling of accounts and the International Investment Bank which promotes "the international socialist division of labour and co-operation of production". Economic co-operation among the member countries is said to have been achieved.

A third possibility may be more feasible. This is for a wider European Community to adopt the principles of a free trade area, leaving the existing Twelve to remain in a customs union if they so wished, while Eastern European countries could continue to have some association with Comecon or to join EFTA. As not all countries might consider it in their interests to remove their barriers, free trade throughout the whole Continent would not necessarily follow. Each country being free to join in the circle of interest if it so wished, all those outside the customs union would retain control over commercial policy. What is important is that countries coming within the circle of interest, by agreeing to membership of a free trade area instead of a customs union, would be doing nothing to damage the economies of countries outside Europe. The formation of what is called the European Economic Space, the linking together of the EC and EFTA, is a step towards this alternative.

The centrepiece of the Community's customs union,

the Common Agricultural Policy, is an extreme form of protectionism. Any form of trade protection may injure people in other countries, but it is now well established that no protectionist policy in the last half century has done more to damage world trade or cause more poverty in the agrarian economies of the Third World than the CAP. Both selfish and aggressive, it has been damaging ecologically as well as to the economic welfare of millions of poor people in the Community itself.

Such strong words ought to be substantiated. The principle of self-sufficiency, almost by definition, is selfish. When good-natured souls seek a rural retreat to provide for themselves as many of their needs as their smallholdings can provide, no harm is done to the world at large; once a whole nation or, worse still, a mega-state of 300 millions declares a policy of self-sufficiency, the consequences for others can be tragic. The Third World is overwhelmingly agrarian; sometimes mining, textiles or tourism may supplement their income, but it is on what their soils can yield that their incomes depend. There is no farmer anywhere in the world who will try to earn a livelihood from his land by spending a year of his life tilling his fields, nurturing his crops and eventually harvesting them unless he first of all is confident that the crops he harvests will find a purchaser at a reasonable price. Of the hundreds of millions of farmers in the world, there is no exception to that. Efficient low-cost producers of food in over fifty countries of the world have seen the Common Agricultural Policy, in applying the principle of Community Preference, put up levies, quotas, prohibitions and other barriers to prevent consumers in the Community from buying their food. Most of the poorest victims have been in West Africa where farmers in their thousands are surrounded by vast areas of good quality land, capable of growing maize, rice, sugar and numerous other crops, yet a great proportion of it

87

lies uncultivated. Worse still, is the sight of thousands of men, women and children in a state of desperate hunger; they hunger because they have no money to buy food; they have no money because they have no work, and there is no work because their agrarian economy cannot export. If European consumers were allowed to buy this food, the farmer, then assured of a market, would begin the laborious year's work in producing it; then, confident of an income, the producer could afford to employ others, paying them an income which in turn would be spent on food.

In the case of rice, for example, as it is grown in Italy it becomes a "Community product", and import levies are imposed to protect its growers. These vary but in round figures they are usually about £100 per tonne. Low-cost producers in the Third World can often overcome such a tariff, but once the rice is semi-milled, the levy is doubled; when wholly-milled another 50% may be added. Yet the process of milling the rice provides many more jobs in the Third World producing countries; for the EC to double or triple the import tax on the rice is effectively to exclude great quantities from the European market. The consumers pay a price for the rice far in excess of what they would in conditions of free trade, and many tens of thousands of poor people lose their employment and, therefore, an income to buy food for themselves and their children.

When Winston Churchill, forming a government in 1940, invited Dr. Dalton to be Minister for Economic Warfare, he described his job as preventing the merchant ships transporting cargoes to enemy ports. Protectionism may not resort to the torpedo, but it does exactly what Dr. Dalton was enjoined to do. By damaging the economic welfare of another country, it cannot avoid causing resentment and friction, which in turn brings retaliation, and so a trade war begins. Our Victorian forbears had a toast: "Peace and Free Trade with all the world." The two go together, and historians have difficulty in thinking of an instance of a shooting war having broken out between two countries that had been freely trading together.

It is, though, the ecological case for free trade that should now come to the fore; and in particular so far as the production of food and the natural fibres of wool and cotton are concerned. A customs union, with the protectionist principle of Community Preference as its centrepiece, inevitably will do more damage to the world's ecology than a free trade area. Modern methods of agriculture, which promote high input/high output systems of food production, make protectionism even more damaging to the world's finite resources.

The whole purpose of protectionism is to change the venue of food production from where it is economically the most efficient to where it is less so. Efficiency is measured in terms of monetary cost, but there are strong grounds for showing that as this rises so does the ecological cost. The farmer's first monetary cost relates to his land, either the price at which he buys it or his rent. When the Corn Laws of the early 19th Century were protecting England's agriculture, there was great distress among farmers which led David Ricardo in his *Theory of Rent* to demonstrate the fallacy of protection. As the tax on imported corn went up, so did the value of corn-growing land at home; higher rents were then charged and the increase in rent equalled the rise in the price of corn, leaving the farmer, if a tenant, no better off. Exactly the same process has happened since the UK conformed to the Common Agricultural Policy. The value of agricultural land has risen at a rate far greater than inflation. To calculate the difference between what the price of farmland would be now had it risen in line with inflation and its actual value today is not difficult; nor is it difficult to calculate the difference between what the cost of food to consumers would have been over the same period, if they had been allowed to buy on the world market, and the actual cost they have paid. The two totals come to the same figure. It is not a mere coincidence. To raise artificially the value of a product must have the effect of raising the value of the asset which produces that product, and as the product goes up in value so does the asset. Competition to take advantage of the artificial price will ensure that all the additional value of the product will be transferred to the value of the asset. When the product is food, and the asset land, the landowner sees his property worth more and the farmer as a food producer finds himself forced to get his fields to yield a higher income. The hedgerows are then seen by him in a different light. Harbouring rabbits that eat his corn, or taking up valuable space, they are ripped up to grow something saleable, so in the UK 190,000 miles of hedgerows are lost. The ancient woodlands likewise serve no purpose, so 50 per cent of them have been destroyed in recent years. The pasture meadows which were a mix of many grasses and wild flowers, cannot sustain as many cattle and sheep as reseeded leys, so 97 per cent of them have gone. Of our chalk grasslands, 80 per cent have given way to the plough. Too often the farmer is criticised for this vandalism; but it is the policy of protectionism that makes him ruthless, forcing him to raise output year after year, and to make that his paramount concern.

The chemist, or rather the chemical company, has added to the bulldozer other aids for the farmer in his quest for more production. The use of nitrates, and the evolution of new crop varieties to absorb greater quantities of nitrogen, have been the main factors in enabling wheat yields to double, and then quadruple, and double yet again in the future. To grow four tons on the same acre that grew one ton thirty years ago verges upon the miraculous. But the nitrate levels in our water supply are also rising beyond what the World Health Organisation considers safe; quite apart from human health, the excess nitrogen is claimed by ecologists to have had an adverse effect upon plant life in our rivers and streams as well as on the fish and other forms of wild life. The other artificial fertiliser now used, phosphate, is claimed by a group of German scientists to be a cause of unnatural aggression when ingested by humans. Then there are pesticides; by definition they kill. The pest to the food producer is still part of nature's kingdom in which every predator has itself a predator, so the death of a herb, fungus, insect, aphid, worm or other pest to the farmer is a loss of food to something else; and as the latter, whether bird, insect or mammal, must diminish in number with the loss of food supply, so must another range of predators suffer. Scientists acknowledge there is a limit to the number of chemical compounds that can be formed into pesticides. As a pest becomes immune, so another generation of pest-killers has to be found, invariably more potent than the previous one, so the chain of death grows longer.

There is another reason for concern. Many of the resources used for modern food production are finite. There is a limit to the quantity of oil for use as fuel in tractors and combines or for making into nitrate fertilisers. There is a limit on the quantity of phosphates that can be mined; and there is a limit to the number of chemical compounds that can become pesticides. Every part of every piece of plant and machinery on the farm is also made from a finite resource. Yet, as we are often reminded, the world's population is far from remaining finite in size. If in the 21st Century the additional billions of humans are to have food to eat, it seems not unreasonable to argue that the finite resources necessary to feed them should be used as economically as possible. In conditions of universal free trade that is what happens, for each country produces what it can at the lowest economic cost. Economic cost and ecological cost seemingly correspond. The factors of agricultural production are never quite the same in any two countries (and, purists would say, not even on any two adjoining farms). Above all, the quality of land varies; and if the finite resource of land is to be used to the most economical advantage for the purpose of feeding the greatest number of people, it follows that the land with the most suitable soil, climate and terrain for the growing of a particular crop or keeping particular types of animals should be the kind used. Whether it is in country A or country B should not be a consideration. But a customs union does exacly that: it stipulates that because country A is inside the protected union, the people living there should be induced by tariffs, quotas, prohibitions and other means to eat what country A produces in preference to what may be imported from country B, although the latter will be using fewer of the world's finite resources.

The quality of land in country A is likely to deteriorate if over a period of time its farmers are induced to go on forcing it to yield more. Soil erosion is the outcome. Desertification, an ugly word for an ugly happening, is accelerating in every continent; millions of acres have been transformed from rich fertility to an arid waste by *homo sapiens;* and it goes on faster now than ever, despite history telling us that past civilisations perished because of it. No soil; no life. The axiom is lost on a rapidly expanding urban society whose ever-increasing demands for food cannot be met through good husbandry: monoculture takes over and soil erosion begins; slowly at first but later speeding up suddenly until the point of no return is reached. Is it possible for what happened in Egypt or Babylonia long ago or in Oklahoma not so long ago, to happen also in Europe? The UK Soil Survey, an official body, has found that the arable farms of Bedfordshire are losing their soil at a rate of one ton per acre per year. At that rate, this not untypical county will not be worth cultivating at some time in the 21st Century.

Soil erosion is not an unnatural process; even well farmed land may lose up to ¾ ton an acre a year, but good husbandry is capable of replacing it by more than that. First there is the farmyard manure put on as fertiliser: this not only breaks down to become soil but acts as a food supply to the worms and other creatures which make the soil. But intensive arable farming requires nitrates instead which do nothing to replace lost soil. Every tree and every yard of hedgerow may have thousands of leaves to fall in the autumn and every particle of them is capable of forming soil. But modern farming is ridding itself of trees and hedges. Then the pesticides are applied; these kill off the worms and the other creatures (and over a million microbes may live in a tablespoonful of healthy soil) which are nature's agents as earth manufacturers, transforming rock and clay into what can sustain higher forms of life. Then along comes *homo sapiens* with modern machinery too dangerous to use along the contours of the landscape, so plying its way up the hill it leaves behind a channel for the heavy rainfall to sweep away the soil to the ditch and thence in a muddy flow to the river and eventually out to sea. Many millions of pounds of public money have been paid in drainage grants to widen and deepen the ditches and so place no hindrance to the soil being washed away. Hence the net loss of soil which ultimately, unless the policy is changed, brings disaster.

What it comes to is this. When a customs union imposed a regime of agricultural protectionism in years past, consumers would pay more for their food and other countries would have their economies damaged, but ecologically it was of little consequence. Today it is quite different. Modern farming, with the technology of chemical inputs and elaborate machinery, gives the farmer the ability to increase food production on land that nature has decreed to be less suitable for the purpose than other land. It is not impossible for a member country in a free trade area to raise protectionist barriers against third countries but it can also refuse to do so. In a customs union, founded upon the principle of Community Preference, a member country can have no alternative but to contribute to this kind of ecological damage.

Finally there is the point about "sovereignty". It has only been with difficulty that all the Twelve have accepted the supranational nature of the Community's customs union. Britain especially is still not reconciled to all its consequences. Every customs union makes it necessary for a member country to agree to a common commercial policy, in a way which a free trade area does not. A prospective member will therefore detect a disadvantage in joining; and whatever degree of hesitation may be prompted, it remains something of a disincentive. Those who believe in a deeper Europe will not cavil at it. But if Europe is seen as a continent of thirty five countries in many circles of interest, the fewer the obstacles put in the way of them working together within those circles, the sooner we will advance towards a Community called Europe equated with the geographical reality.

6

Some Overlapping Circles

At last, after years of exertion by a small number of writers and scientists, there is an awakening to the dangers besetting our planet. As no one country can contract out of the consequences, policies globally agreed are the obvious objective, but not all the environmental problems are global: some are regional, others concern a limited number of neighbouring countries, while a few are national. If the policies proposed are to succeed, they have to be appropriate for each of these categories. That should be a statement of the obvious. Policies, however, are being sought for regional problems when the problems are limited to only a few of the countries in a region. This indeed is what the EC is attempting to do. It is entirely appropriate for the EC to consider a common policy for its region of the Twelve, provided that each problem is one that concerns all the Twelve and only them. Otherwise it is doubtful whether the EC is the appropriate body to formulate common policies in this sphere of action. The EC Commission itself sees the dilemma; and the European Environmental Agency which it has set up is to explore the environmental issues for all Europe. This welcome move is to take the form initially of gathering data from all European countries. The only criticism to be made about that is that the Economic Commission for Europe is already engaged in this activity, its first efforts in this field going back to 1957. A duplication of effort seems pointless, and it might be said that the whole range of these issues is better left with the ECE, which has, as a later chapter shows, an excellent record in co-ordinating international action.

Nothing was said about the environment in the Treaty of Rome. When the EC Commission published its report *Ten Years of Community Environment Policy* in 1984 it began:

> "If twenty-seven years ago, when the European Community was founded, one had spoken of the environment, people would no doubt have thought that one was referring either to the climate or to the state of business confidence."

Since then the Single European Act ratified in 1987 has amended the Treaty to include Article 130R(2) which states "Environmental protection requirements shall be a component of the Community's other policies." This gives the Commissioner responsible for the environment a voice in all its business. It also makes the Community a supranational authority in the matter of the environment. Some will see this as a desirable advance and a means of getting the laggards into line with the countries with higher standards. Britain, often denounced as one of the culprits, will then be forced to mend her ways to the advantage of her own people as well as others. But it may not work out like this. The EC's supranational authority depends upon how the Council of Ministers exercises its powers of legislation. As this is by majority voting, it does not follow that the countries with the higher standards will have enough votes to enforce them upon the laggards. The chances are that it will be the other way about. This bodes ill for progress.

The trouble with environmental policy, as with almost every other aspect of policy, is that there is not enough convergence of interest among the Twelve for all to agree amicably upon a new policy, and — which is more important — to enforce that new policy in their own countries. If Europe is to have appropriate policies for the environment, they will have to come from appropriate groupings of countries, which necessarily means groups that are in circles of common interest. Fine words butter no parsnips, as the saying goes, and fine words enshrined in a common policy about any environmental issue agreed in Brussels will achieve nothing unless the member governments have the determination to enforce it. It is true that the Commission may take an offending country to the European Court of Justice, but even when the country has had a series of warnings over a period of years, and the Court has found against its government, it cannot be compelled to enforce the policy unless it has the will to do so.

The experience of the Commission has shown how difficult its task is. After the Stockholm Convention of 1972 its First Action Programme was agreed by the Council of Ministers; it set out a four year plan on a number of environmental concerns; and sadly it was a failure. Then came the Second Action Programme in 1977, also for four years, but this was little more than a regurgitation of the first one. So then came the Third Action Programme in 1983, again for four years. This time it was slightly different, and an emphasis was placed upon integrating an environmental element into other policies, yet the years went by and words were more pronounced than action. So then came the Fourth Action Programme in 1987, yet again for four years. Whether

97

this will be any more successful than its predecessors is doubtful. Sadly there is little sign of the parsnips being buttered by the fine words of any of the four programmes. They have, however, added to the debate and they have made an important contribution to the thinking in many government departments among the Twelve, besides helping to stir up public opinion. Their success in the debate, though, is outweighed by a failure in action. It demonstrates how the supranational approach requires supranational powers of coercion. Yet ought such powers of coercion to be exercised over a minority of countries that are outside the appropriate circle?

The disaster at Chernobyl, perhaps more than any other event, brought home to Europe how fragile is the continent. A minor (in nuclear terms) explosion three years ago has still made sheep grazing in North Wales unfit to eat. How many thousands of people will die as a result of the radiation will never be known. What we do know is that Europe has become environmentally a small place. But a Europe-wide policy by which the standards of the highest become the norm is not feasible for the reason that some of the poorest countries, particularly in Eastern Europe, are the worst polluters, and their poverty denies them the means of raising their standards. This makes it necessary to consider two kinds of circles of interest — circles of countries that share an environmental interest, which are divided into further circles for those able to pay for what has to be done and those unable to do so.

Before looking at those circles, let us consider some of the ones already in existence in other areas.

Patents

To anyone enthused with a vision of a United States of Europe, putting patents — as dull and pedestrian a topic as most of us can imagine — as the first of the circles of interest will raise at least a derisory eyebrow. Of course, it is not the most important circle and in any order of merit it can safely go down the list. It is placed first to underline three things. A common patent policy exists in Europe — a Europe that includes Sweden, Austria and Switzerland — and has done so for many years with immense benefit to the people of Europe. On the principle that no news is good news we never read a word about its achievements because they never seem to cause the kind of friction and dispute that the media will report so readily. Secondly, prosaic though it may be, the common policy on patents points to the kind of international co-operation where the prospects for advance are most favourable, namely in areas of technology. Technology is far from dull to technologists; and with one voice they say there are still greater strides forward to be made in Europe, both in and out of the EC and in both small countries and large. The most important point about the European patent policy is that it shows how successfully a policy can be managed over many years when the right mechanisms are adopted, international and not supranational.

A single application to the European Patent Office in Munich can be enough to obtain a patent for any invention to take effect throughout most of the Continent. Thus there is now no necessity to travel around the capitals taking out a series of patents. One can still, if so desired, obtain a patent for a limited number of countries, but the reduced fee offers little inducement to do so. This splendid piece of practical internationalism has come about "by convention". Each country subscribing to the European Patent Office has entered into a treaty to make the system work and the legislature of each of the separate countries has enacted laws giving effect to the treaty. The laws are harmonised, so that for all practical purposes inventors, engineers, scientists and business-men throughout most of Europe have the same rights and obligations in the matter of patents; and disputes are settled centrally in the EPO. Within a very wide circle, the interests of a great number of individuals in many different countries have converged together, and their national parliaments have done something very worthwhile to protect them. No minority has been coerced; no argument has been heard; it has all gone very smoothly, and the national parliaments have acted in harmony with one another because the laws themselves which they passed were in harmony with the interests of the people.

Non-Tariff Barriers

Some years ago when GATT tried to identify all the non-tariff barriers which existed its experts went as far as compiling a list of no less than forty-four different classes of these barriers; and they had to give up the task of going further for there seemed to be no limit to human ingenuity in devising new forms of self-protection in trade. Some of them begin honestly enough — the health regulations, for example, which prohibit imports of products carrying disease — but in due course there is a temptation to stretch the meaning of the words and the cargo returns to its port of origin. Officials in the Commission have done valiant work in trying to check this ingenuity, sometimes successfully, but usually to little avail. A country sets up a non-tariff barrier because it believes it is in its interest to do so. In other words it indicates by its action that it desires to withdraw from particular circles of interest.

Trying to bring all these barriers to an end throughout the Community may be laudable, but it manifestly goes against what some countries in some circumstances wish to see done. As it is, the Commission, having identified a

100

particular type of trade barrier and believing the Council of Ministers may approve legislation to bring it to an end, will put before the ministers a draft directive or regulation. Not wishing to appear lacking in Community spirit, each minister may agree to the draft. But its enforcement remains initially a matter for national action, so if a government decides to overlook the new legislation the Commission can do little about it unless another country complains (which it may be reluctant to do in case it proves to be also an offender) or the breach is so blatant that the Commission may take the offending country to the European Court of Justice.

In a partnership of nation-states the Commission could have a lesser though more effective role to play. Acting either on their own initiative or on the suggestion of a member country, the Commissioners could select a trade barrier which one or more countries may have introduced which has stifled commerce between them. It could then in its role as a secretariat arrange a conference between the countries to put forward proposals for an agreement on the basis of a *quid pro quo*. A common interest being forged, the likelihood of the barriers being brought down and the countries enforcing the change in good faith would be great. This alternative may have to be adopted if the objective of the single market, which is effectively the elimination of non-tariff barriers, fails to be achieved.

Anti-Dumping Rules

Dumping takes two forms; either it is at the expense of the exporter himself or it is subsidised by the government. The former is seldom serious and rarely continues for long. Any exporter minded to undercut his competitors by trading at a loss may capture a market in this way, but experience shows that this manoeuvre usually affords only a temporary benefit, and the cost can break even a major company.

Dumping with taxpayers' money is another story. The present anti-dumping procedure introduced by the EC works so slowly that it often gives no protection to the victim; especially in the case of horticultural products. A new policy is proposed but it will still require an application to the Commission and consequent delay. The UK's anti-dumping law worked with reasonable success before she entered the EC and no-one suggests it was less effective than the system now. If a country cannot decide for itself when its own industries are threatened by dumping, it is not altogether easy to think of what it can decide for itself. If over one hundred and fifty other countries have their own anti-dumping laws, it might be appropriate if the United Kingdom, as well as the other countries in the EC, were to join them.

Other Policies Relating to a Single Market

There is much to be done in the field — too much if we are to envisage a truly single market among twelve countries with economies that vary so considerably. Moreover, their existing laws differ so enormously that any speedy harmonisation may well cause an injury to minorities whose interests could be overlooked. The United Kingdom has attached great importance to a single market for banking and financial services, but what happens in most of the countries in northern Europe is very different from that prevailing in the south. More real progress might be made if the United Kingdom and those other countries in northern Europe which had somewhat similar practices about banking and financial services were to initiate their own common rules, and once these were working and seemed to be successful to enable other countries in Europe to adhere to them.

Concorde

Taxpayers were entitled to murmur about the cost of Concorde, but only the most churlish failed to salute the amazing advance in aeronautics. Two ancient rivals sat down at the table, agreed that neither of them could afford such a venture on their own, but together it was feasible, provided they could work together. The two governments invited respective legislatures to authorise the expenditure and the work got under way. A simple piece of international co-operation duly gave birth to the wonder of modern travel. Brussels, so far as we know, was not consulted. Moreover, so far as we know, no disagreements erupted. If it is ever true that there may be times in the future when a modern industry may be too costly for a single European country, Concorde provides a precedent likely to cause less bother than any plan by a supranational Commission to coax twelve into line.

Coal and Steel

Coal and steel are two of the declining industries that were given a fresh lease of life; and in Britain both have been so rejuvenated as to make them candidates for private ownership. The credit, it is said, must go to the European Coal and Steel Community; by exercising its supranational powers it has forced the pace at which these two industries have been slimmed down and made competitive.

The inference is that unless those supranational powers had been used, the coal and steel industries would still be in a state of decline. It is a claim that the leaders of the two industries in both Britain and other parts of the Community would hesitate to accept, and it is a reflection upon the massive efforts that they have made to reorganise the corporations they have been responsible for. In the first place, both coal and steel are fundamental to any developed industrial country; for it to allow either to remain in a state of decline would be a burden too great to leave alone. Major surgery was a patent necessity for both coal and steel, and would have been carried out regardless of whether it were decreed by an external authority. Countries outside the Community also with an excess capacity of coal or steel have been seen to do no less for their industries than those inside.

But supranationality is the wrong kind of weapon to wield. The power is superfluous when a country is in trouble except for the purpose of getting a national government to do what it would not otherwise do in its own interest. A group of governments faced with a common problem, with representatives meeting together to reach a solution to it, will try to agree among themselves; and if they succeed the presence of a superior authority is not called for. If, however, they fail to agree it will be because at least one of the representatives present is convinced that it is not in the interests of his country to do so. The entry then of a superior authority may become useful, but its usefulness will be measured by its power of coercing the minority to agree. What goes for coal and steel must hold for any major industry in decline. An inter-governmental agreement to put matters right, or as right as it can, will cause the least injustice.

Western European Union

Five countries, France, The Netherlands, Belgium, Luxembourg and the United Kingdom were represented when the Treaty of Brussels was signed in 1948. The Treaty provided for the collective defence of the five countries and their collaboration over social, economic and cultural matters. Although the provisions for

defence were later transferred to NATO, the economic
ones to the EC and the remaining matters to the Council
of Europe, the WEU still exists; and its Assembly, the
membership being drawn from the national parliaments, meets in parallel with the Council of Europe.

The French government, being detached or semi-
detached from NATO (no-one seems sure which it is),
from time to time expresses the view that the WEU
should be reactivated as a defence treaty for Western
Europe, and this may well be in the interests of the
United States, now that she has hinted more than once
that her role in NATO may diminish. An enlarged WEU
incorporating the other NATO countries of Europe
would be an advantage to the UK in that an agreement
could then be reached as to how much each country
would spend on defence. At present the UK's burden on
a *per capita* basis related to GDP far exceeds that borne by
Western Germany, so this reassessment appears overdue. Furthermore, a great part of this expenditure by the
UK is on preparation not for home defence, but that of
Western Germany.

There may be a powerful case for the British people to
have more regard for the defence of their own country;
indeed Peter Johnson in *Neutrality: a Policy for Britain* has
made a suprisingly strong case for Britain disentangling
herself from any alliance. However, so long as the UK in
matters of defence sees herself in a circle of interest which
includes a number of other countries, both inside and
outside the European Community, the WEU is there in
place as a vehicle to be used.

Defence procurement has been spoken of as another
function for the EC. That advantages may be gained by
countries sharing out among themselves the business of
manufacturing weapons is obvious enough in any area of
high-cost defence technology. It is less obvious that the
task can be undertaken satisfactorily by the EC. For all

105

the countries in the alliance to take part in the common policy in defence procurement would seem more appropriate. Accordingly Norway would be inside the circle, the Republic of Ireland outside.

The Alps

In turning now to the environmental issues, let us single out the Alps for particular attention. This range of magnificent mountains in the heart of Europe, the inspiration of so much of European art, music and literature, is steadily being transformed into a lifeless desert of rock. The millions of trees that have held the soil and snow for thousands of years are being killed off by pollution, one forest after another dying and then rotting or being carried away either by man or more frequently floodwater. Once the trees go, soil erosion follows. The tens of thousands of farmers who maintained the protective range of trees and did much else to enhance the beauty of the Alps by a gentle form of husbandry are leaving, their form of farming no longer able to afford them a livelihood. But the winter sportsmen, walkers and mountaineers grow in number, now exceeding forty million a year, and each one adds to the soil eroded and lost, so it is now only a matter of time before the Alps will have changed to something which will give Europeans neither pride nor pleasure. No longer safe for skiers, no haven for its wildlife, no soil to support the pastures, no place for anyone to work, the Alps will be a wasteland.

Of course, it is not too late to save them. But seven nation-states share the range: France, Switzerland, Italy, Austria, Yugoslavia, Western Germany and Liechtenstein. For success each should have a part in the programme of recovery; and together they must find many hundreds of millions of pounds to pay for what needs to be done. An international effort is obvious.

106

Is it not a role for a refashioned European Community which enables Switzerland, Austria, Yugoslavia and Liechtenstein to join? The circle of interest comprising seven countries would be formed to decide the action to be taken; and perhaps, in this special case, an outer circle of other European countries could be formed to contribute to the vast expenditure the programme will entail.

Energy Conservation

Although everyone can do something to reduce the waste of energy, a national, as well as an international, effort is required to achieve success in putting right the "global warming". Now that we know the main cause is due to carbon dioxide, we ought to heed the conclusion reached by the American Carbon Dioxide Information Centre at Oak Ridge National Laboratory. The emission of carbon dioxide, it claims, in the United Kingdom is steadily rising by 2.6% a year; in 1987 it reached 156 million tonnes, and there seem to be comparable increases throughout most of northern Europe.

The Independent carried out a study on the extent the average family could reasonably be expected to conserve energy, which it published in its issue for July 3rd 1989. It reached the conclusion that by itself a family could not achieve very much. A family consisting of a married couple with two children living in a semi-detached house on the outskirts of a Midlands town was chosen as average. They owned a 1.6 litre car which went 10,000 miles a year; the father, however, travelled 10 miles to work daily by train; one child went to school 2 miles away by bus; and for their main holiday, the car was left behind as they flew to the Mediterranean seaside. Gas was used for their central heating. To establish their use of energy, the study relied upon the advice of British Gas, the Electricity Council, the Energy Technology Support

Unit and a number of individual experts as well as using the statistics of the Departments of Transport and Energy.

Through the burning of fossil fuels this typical family produced 44 tonnes of carbon dioxide a year, a little more than the national average of 10.2 tonnes per person each year. The study showed that only 13.9 tonnes of their 44 tonnes was under their personal control and it would be difficult to make a major inroad into that one-third. 5.6 tonnes was attributable to the family's central heating, at 40 per cent the largest contributor to their production of carbon dioxide. One tonne of this could be reduced if home insulation and an expensive condensing boiler were put in; this is less than might be expected because gas produces less carbon dioxide than oil or coal. Petrol for their car will cause three times its body weight of gas to pollute the air every year, and this 3.5 tonnes could no doubt be reduced; but only half a tonne would be saved by the family using the bus as much as practicable instead of the car and a tonne by forgoing a holiday flight. The family's electricity accounted for another 3.3 tonnes. Any saving here has a useful knock-on effect as no less than two-thirds of the energy from the fossil fuels, coal and oil, used at the power station are lost in the cooling towers or in transmission. The share of carbon dioxide of four passengers flying to and from their holiday, with the aircraft travelling at 500 mph is just one tonne.

Were every family to reduce its energy consumption by one-third, the national saving would be only one-tenth. The great effort needed and the consequent fall in the convenience and comfort of the whole population has to be set against a saving far short of what is desirable. If that annual national average of 44 tonnes per head is to be reduced we must look to industry, public transport, the airlines and government, both local and national, each to make changes of policy.

The changes could cost British industry many billions of pounds. This can be found by government subsidies, reductions in company taxation or raising prices to the consumer. The burden may be justified and worthwhile, but what if others in Europe sit on their hands and do nothing? No one country can be expected to act by itself; whilst the unfairness to industry in becoming less competitive might be offset by government aid, the success of any change of policy will turn on how many of the countries responsible for this pollution contribute to its decrease in an equitable manner. For this some kind of international agreement may be reached. Ideally, one would wish for every country on our planet to be a party to it. A global policy may come one day, but it is more realistic to expect co-operation from the leading industrial nations in the region that is the source of most of the pollution. The latter is, of course, Europe; and Poland and the Soviet Union are among those nations, together with Western Germany, France, Italy and the UK. Although it would be desirable for all countries in Europe to march together in this battle, the difficulties and the consequent delay might be considerable, and immediate assembly of a circle of interests comprising the larger industrial nations seems more likely to succeed.

Acid Rain

This allied problem also embraces in a circle of interest countries both inside and outside the Community. No one doubts the urgency of the problem and there is now some agreement about how it can be overcome. Yet no steps are taken, nor are likely to be, by the Community, as its membership fails to coincide with the circle of interested countries. Progress seems more prob-

109

able under the wings of the Economic Commission for Europe.

The North Sea

In November 1989, the eight countries adjacent to the North Sea met in London to consider what should be done to save it from ecological death. The pressures upon it have been severe and can only be reversed by a major effort against the flow of pollutants from each of the eight countries. The conference was the initiative of the UK government; and as not all the countries are in the EC, any legislation or revenue for the common policy will have to be decided internationally.

Food Safety

As the marketing of many kinds of food across the frontiers is going to increase, agreed standards of food safety will become of still greater importance than they are today. This desirable objective can easily be thwarted by a lack of enforcement on the part of national authorities or by standards set too low. The regulations about food hygiene throughout most of southern Europe are either very few or observed so cavalierly as to be of little consequence. While it is easy to cast stones at their casual regard for the health of others, it might be added that it is borne of the knowledge that their produce has been traditionally sold and eaten locally, while in the main still fresh. Thus the standards of northern Europe were not quite so necessary. The EC in its attempts to regulate matters of food safety is unlikely to raise standards to those of the highest. As anyone who has seen what goes on in parts of Greece, Italy and Spain would accept, it would be intolerable if the standards of the UK, which are not even the highest, were brought down to their level. Yet to expect them to agree to, let alone enforce, our laws to make them change their ways

110

is to be rather too optimistic. In the UK we have more than a hundred regulations about food hygiene; Germany, The Netherlands, Denmark, Norway, Sweden and Finland have a similar number; and it would be feasible to make these the same, and perhaps Ireland, France, Belgium and Luxembourg will be willing to accept them.

Under the heading of food safety comes the subject of pesticides. The two agencies of the UN, the World Health Organisation and the Food and Agriculture Organisation, having failed to promote any world-wide control of their use, it looks as if any international action will have to be in regional terms. The highest standards are in Scandinavia, where it has been agreed that no pesticide should be used unless it is shown to be neither a danger to human health nor damaging to the environment. As pesticides, by definition, are killers of pests, most doctors, especially those who have in their care farmers, gardeners, foresters, groundsmen and other frequent users, recognise the potential chronic risk that pesticides create. The House of Commons Select Committee on Agriculture held an eighteen-month inquiry on the question and those members who had heard all the evidence were agreed that there could be no doubt about the serious dangers and that changes in the law were clearly necessary. However, the chemical and pharmaceutical industries, to safeguard their interests, set up lobbies in Brussels; their influence may or may not have dissuaded the Commission from introducing legislation more effective than that which we already have; certainly there is no sign of the Commission wishing to adopt the more rigorous regulations of the Nordic countries. The UK, Western Germany and France each have very large and powerful pesticide manufacturers with worldwide connections, which make it less likely that either the Community or those three countries individually will do

111

much more about pesticides. Progress may therefore
depend upon other countries in Europe, particularly in
the east, following the example of Scandinavia and
perhaps becoming associated with the Nordic Council
for the purpose of keeping the regulations up to date and
approving new pesticides as they are made available.

Is it fair to make it a criminal offence for a farmer or
grower to use a particular pesticide which may make a
crop more profitable to produce than otherwise, while
permitting imports from a country which allows his competitors to use them? Logic suggests that the two prohibitions should proceed in tandem.

If no advance can be made in regulating the use of
pesticides, at least much could be done to harmonise the
research into their use and dangers. Their cost to the farmer gets greater every year, yet the spraying equipment
of every farmer causes much more to be used than
necessary. Research in recent years has made some valuable improvements, but more can be done. As neither
the WHO nor the FAO is able or willing to take a lead
over this, an opportunity arises for a number of governments to pool resources and co-ordinate their
research.

Government agencies in the UK, US and Canada, to a
limited extent, exchange information about the safety of
pesticides. Whether they are considered safe or not
depends almost entirely upon their effect on animals.
The scientific validity of this research is open to doubt
and numerous examples can be given of where tests on
animals have led us astray, the tests on thalidomide being
the most notorious example. Tens of thousands of
animals, mainly rats and mice, but also dogs, cats, mon-
keys and others, are submitted to these tests, and with the
LD50 test they may be given the chemical till they die.
The total amount of animal suffering is quite considerable, but since each country carries out its own tests, the

duplication is enormous. The case for this work being done internationally seems irrefutable, but would France, Germany and the UK, each with a major pesticide manufacturer in strong competition, agree to this? Quite apart from reducing the animal suffering, there could be considerable reduction in cost, so if those three countries are unwilling to agree to a common research programme, there may well be another circle of interest established, consisting of others.

Animal Welfare

As with pesticides, so with farm animals; if one country prohibits meat being produced in a particular way, ought there not to be a further prohibition of that kind of meat being imported from a country that allows that method of production? The UK has made it illegal to rear veal calves in crates so narrow that they cannot turn around. Ironically, however, it has only added to the cruelty, for the tens of thousands of calves that would have been made into veal here are now exported soon after birth to France and The Netherlands, where they are put into crates until slaughtered, then come back here dead to be eaten.

The Commission of the EC has done nothing to improve farm animal welfare, for it is well aware that nothing would be achieved unless the national governments were willing to make sure the regulations were enforced properly. Again, there is a difference to be found between northern and southern Europe. Whether the reason is to be attributed to cultural or religious influences is not a question to be answered easily; what is certain is that as a general rule farm animals in all stages of their life, not least in the slaughter house, are treated worse in southern Europe, and better in the Nordic countries than in the rest of northern Europe. Three circles of interest are apparent. Merge them into one and the standards, both in the law and its enforcement, would be those of the lowest. Half Europe would accordingly step backwards.

Indeed, Denmark is going backwards. Before entering the Community, her laws on animal welfare were as rigorous as any in the world. Among other things, battery cages for egg-laying hens were illegal. That law is no longer in force, for it added to the cost of eggs and once the trade barriers were down, eggs were freely imported from other countries where batteries were permitted, and made available at prices which the Danish poultry farmer could not match.

Ever since fourteen children died in Yorkshire, some twenty years ago, from salmonella poisoning, having failed to respond to antibiotic treatment, we have known the dangers that arise where pigs, poultry and dairy cows are given substantial doses of these drugs. But one cannot keep over a hundred cows in a single building, or a thousand pigs, or ten thousand poultry, unless antibiotics are available, to prevent the spread of fatal diseases. The profitability of intensive methods of rearing pigs and poultry depends upon the speed at which the animals grow; antibiotics have been proved to be growth stimulants and with their use a day-old chick can reach the slaughter weight of 5 lbs in no less than 49 days. Set against this amazing achievement must be the danger to human health if antibiotics are to be used indiscriminately on our farms. We know that there is a limit to the number of compounds that can be used as antibiotics, and one by one they are losing their efficacy. There will come a time when this life-saving resource will no longer be available for human beings. Not for decades may that time come, yet it would be irresponsible not to put a check upon the use of antibiotics as growth stimulants in factory farming. This has been done in the UK, but only to a limited extent, and what is now necessary is an international agreement, incorporating as many countries as feasible. Here the circle of interest encompasses all the countries with factory farming systems similar to our own.

There are numerous aspects of animal husbandry that require regulations both to ensure fair competition and to lessen cruelty. If the regulations are to be respected and enforced across national frontiers, it is plain they ought to be made between nations that have, broadly speaking, the same regard for animal welfare. That regard is not the same throughout all Europe and so long as it differs substantially, any attempt at common laws, enforced equally well in every country, will surely be futile.

Other Environmental Issues

Had the Treaty of Rome never been signed until the later 1980s, the institution's initials might perhaps stand for the European Environmental Community. A lengthy catalogue of environmental issues spanning the frontiers can be drawn up in addition to those listed above. The Commission itself has a list of them on which it has or has attempted a common policy; the pollution of water and air, chemicals, noise, waste, land and natural resources, flora and fauna. A study of what it has achieved and especially what it has failed to achieve shows that the Community is at once too big and yet too small. It is too big to be sensitive to the smaller pockets of environmental concern where local or national action can prove more effective, and it is too small to cope with the numerous concerns that go beyond the boundaries of the Community.

The environmental issues listed already suggest that the supranational action is not the most appropriate. It must begin as the Treaty of Rome describes, by the Commission recognising that a problem exists and then getting down to producing some proposals which are duly placed before the Council of Ministers to approve or reject, with the European Parliament giving its opinion in accordance with the Single European Act. Thus every member-state is included in every decision, regardless of whether it has any interest in the subject. Here lies an immediate danger to any amicable agreement among the countries directly concerned. Let us take the pollution of the Rhine as an example. The countries through which the river passes have a direct interest, for we may assume that pollution is caused by some of their citizens while others have their health, livelihood or recreation put at risk. On balance, it is decided that the rights of the latter outweigh those of the former; the Commission gets to work and eventually legislation is drafted for the Council of Ministers to approve. The governments of the countries primarily affected, having studied the draft, authorise the ministers to approve them. But like most good things, the plans cost money to execute and the Commission proposes in the draft that Community funds should be made available. This may not be to the liking of the other countries which see no advantage to themselves in their money being spent to clean up other people's pollution in a river far from them. Moreover, on the Council of Ministers they are in a majority, so they are tempted to block the progress being made until some other proposal is introduced by the Commission which will give them some benefit. As Christopher Tugendhat said, after eight years experience of the office, being a Commissioner was like being Sisyphus. The poor man, it may be remembered, was condemned to push a heavy stone up a steep hill and each time that he had nearly reached the top it would slip from his hands and fall to the bottom again. It may not take much for the Council of Ministers to reject the draft and for the Commissioners' work to start all over again. When Com-

116

missioners dabble in the noise of lawnmowers it may not matter very much, but other environmental issues can be of desperate urgency. Unless a country finds itself in a circle of interest, only a sense of altruism with which few governments are much endowed will enthuse them with any desire to take part, especially when their taxpayers' money is required. Each environmental issue represents a separate circle of interest; and for every circle of interest a different approach is indispensable for progress to be made.

7

Circles Of Conflict

When the original Six formed the Common Market, twenty-one million of its inhabitants were farmers of one kind or another; agriculture was not only the largest source of employment, it dominated the economy; and to create a common market without a common agricultural policy would have been absurd. Several decades of manufacturing growth and the expansion of the Community to Twelve both give us grounds for considering whether it is time to wind up the agricultural policy.

One of the main objectives of the Common Agricultural Policy, according to the Treaty of Rome, was to make sure the farming community had a reasonable income; and a system of guaranteed prices was the plausible means to this laudable end. Despite vast sums of public money being given to support farm prices, the number of farmers has fallen rapidly. The 21 million in the original Six are now 7 million, so 14 million have manifestly not been supported. Is there then a fallacy in the belief that guaranteed prices can guarantee a reasonable livelihood?

A guaranteed price is meaningless unless taxpayers' money is given to increase the price to above what the consumer is willing to pay, and it therefore implies that extra money from outside the market will flow into an industry. This must have the effect of making the assets of the favoured industry more valuable than they would otherwise be. The principal asset of agriculture being land, it would therefore seem likely that its value would rise if farmers were to receive guaranteed prices. This is, indeed, what has happened in the United Kingdom. We can assess, to the nearest billion pounds at least, how much farmgate prices have risen as a result of the CAP; and we can also estimate how much the value of agricultural land has gone up in real terms in the same period. It is not a coincidence that the two total sums are the same. Richard Cobden in his speeches in the Anti-Corn Law campaign argued that the more corn was taxed the more the price of land, and therefore rents, would go up. It is not a case of history repeating itself so much as an economic law being seen to work. Raise the price of a product artificially by government action and the value of the asset necessary for production will rise so as to nullify the benefit of the artificial price. A policy of price support may help the farmer insofar as he is a landowner, but not as a farmer. In the rest of the EC, the landlord and tenant system scarcely exists, so the effect cannot be seen so starkly.

To achieve the objective of supporting farmers, other means must be found. However, whether farmers should be supported at all is a legitimate question. Grocers, greengrocers, butchers and fishmongers do not receive a penny in subsidy, yet in the business of getting food to the consumer their role is nearly as important. A distinction, however, can be drawn between the farmer and others in the chain of food supply. The latter are all businessmen: it is for them to find a customer willing to pay a price at which they can afford to sell; failing that, they serve no purpose in the economy and accordingly should leave to find a useful role elsewhere. True, a farmer may be a businessman insofar as he is selling food; but in the growing of it, he has also a responsibility to the soil, the landscape and the wildlife. Like any other businessman, he is entitled to maximise his profits, but the pursuit of profit is often incompatible with his responsibility to the soil, landscape and wildlife. In this respect he is a trustee for future generations, a guardian or steward of the countryside. Now if the rest of us want him to forgo some of his profits so that he fulfils this other role, it is not unreasonable for him to ask the public for some compensation. It is on this ground that there is a case for giving the farmer money out of public funds.

Let a few examples be cited of how the support might be given. Farmer Green grows arable crops and his small fields are inconvenient for his machinery and the hedgerows that divide the fields take up valuable space that would otherwise be planted with crops; and besides they also harbour rabbits which eat the crops. To uproot the hedgerows would add several thousand pounds to the value of his farm; but the landscape would be much the poorer for it. In return for continuing to farm with the hedgerows, Farmer Green could enter into an agreement whereby he was paid an appropriate sum by way of compensation. In the case of Farmer Black, the nitrate level in the local water supply is above the level recommended by the World Health Organisation; to eliminate all nitrate use on his land would cause him to lose a considerable sum of money, but that loss could be made good by public funds under an agreement.

To pay farmers for safeguarding the environment was considered to be a rather eccentric idea when it was canvassed in a series of books written by me. It is now,

121

however, accepted in the United Kingdom and to a limited degree in other northern countries in the EC, but so far there is no recognition in the other countries that modern methods of agriculture can do grievous damage to the environment.

It highlights one of the great distinctions between North and South in the EC. Generally speaking, no great damage has yet been done in southern Europe; and not until it is will there be a call for this alternative policy. The other difference is that the range of crops in the Mediterranean countries bears little resemblance to that of northern Europe. Paddy rice, olives, tobacco and citrus fruits are as important for them as wheat, potatoes, sugar-beet, milk and beef are to the other half of the EC. For these two reasons an agricultural policy common to twelve countries with such great differences between them is scarcely practical. What is certain is that any attempt to lay down centrally a list of guaranteed prices would create an obvious conflict of interest. Were each to have a similar soil, climate and terrain and to be able to grow the same kinds of food in conditions of equal competition, the causes of conflict would disappear. As it is, there is no convergence of interest, the necessary precondition for a common policy.

But what of the interests of the consumer? Observers outside the Community sometimes express amazement at how the consumers in the EC have allowed their interests to be relegated to the lowest levels of abasement. After all, when millions of tons of food — fruit and vegetables especially — are wilfully destroyed in order to create a shortage and a consequent rise in the price, it may not be totally impertinent to ask whether the purpose of growing this food is for it to be consumed by a human being.

The consumer's interest is best met by freedom of choice, so that food at the lowest price can be purchased and also food of the favourite kind eaten. That plainly means the freedom to buy in the world market. This runs counter to the very core of the Common Agricultural Policy, which is the principle of Community Preference. This requires the consumer to be induced, by means of taxation or prohibition, to buy food produced from within the Community in preference to what he or she might wish to have from outside. The very principle is hostile to the consumer and is a denial of freedom. The taxation is twofold. Food imported from outside the Community is taxed in the form of import levies to make it artificially more expensive, and the consumer, as tax-payer, pays the cost of subsidies to farmers to reduce artificially the price of Community-produced food. Such is the wide gap between the cost of food in the world market and in the Common Market that the two forms of taxation put a severe burden upon the ordinary family. It ought to go without saying that any form of taxation represents a transfer of purchasing power from the tax-payer to the state and a consequent loss of freedom of choice. When the state arrogates to itself the business of spending the citizen's money, it does not follow that it will be spent as he or she would wish. Left in the citizen's pocket there is some certainty it would be spent differently. Of course, it is right that the state should, to some extent, take away this freedom from the citizen. But in the matter of food can we not assume that the citizen, as consumer, knows best what he or she would like to eat?

Food is, if nothing else is, a personal concern. To lay down rules for 300 millions seems to be taking the cause of centralisation further than logic allows. Nor is it realis tic to plan centrally the market for something so unplannable as the supply and demand of food. Who can tell what the weather will do? A heavy rainfall in one month may benefit one crop but devastate another. A small rise

in the price of beef one Friday may cause a million consumers to prefer lamb or pork or poultry meat, or go
vegetarian. Those wise men in Brussels cannot predict
the unpredictable.

A small country may have some hope of being able to
devise and impose an agricultural policy to satisfy both
producer and consumer. Norway, it is sometimes said, is
such a country. It is homogeneous enough to succeed.
To attempt the same for the Twelve in such a way as to
satisfy the Athenian and the Aberdonian is neither practical nor desirable. It is not in the interests of the farmer
and manifestly not of the consumer.

Perhaps (the cynic might add) the great chemical companies which have spent so much money advertising the
merits of the Common Agricultural Policy see it differently. They certainly seem to have done rather well out of a
system which goaded farmers to increase output year
after year and thus caused them to buy ever more of their
products (nitrates, pesticides, hormones, etc.) from those
companies as each year went by. It seems we come back
yet again to the central question: Whose interests are
more important to us? The interests of ordinary people
do not necessarily coincide with those who exercise
power over them.

The other circle which is attempted and which is
unlikely to be beneficial, except to a minority, concerns
the control of our currency. Let us take two neighbouring
countries, Richland and Poorland, both independent
and having therefore separate currencies and governments with control over them. Richland is strongly
industrialised, its capital a financial centre of international importance, and its people able to afford a high
standard of living; Poorland, on the other hand, tends to
import most of its manufactured goods, with a large part
of its population employed in declining industries or on
the land. Richland being a net exporter, and Poorland a

net importer, the latter could soon be a debtor nation. By
retaining control over exchange rates, the government of
Poorland has the power to allow its currency to float
freely, so if her imports from Richland increase or her
exports to Richland decline, the value of her currency is
adjusted immediately. The importer in Poorland soon
discovers this to his cost. In order to buy from Richland
he has to effect the purchase in Richland's currency of
dollars, and to do so he sells shillings, the currency of
Poorland, which is done on his behalf in the foreign
exchange market in order to buy Richland dollars. If
more goods cross the frontier into Poorland than they do
into Richland, the demand for Richland's dollars will go
up and for Poorland's shillings will likewise go down.
Thus every day the price of the two currencies will be
adjusted in accordance with the law of supply and
demand, the dollar steadily rising and the shilling
falling.

A floating exchange rate is sometimes said to be the
most perfect of import controls. It works immediately,
there being no delay which can build up to a crisis with a
major devaluation as the outcome; it also requires no
administration for the hidden hand of market forces
does all that is necessary to make the change in the rate;
and it can never single out any particular importer or
exporter for arbitrary treatment. However, it does make
for some uncertainty and so, in practice, governments
have been persuaded to engineer what is called a dirty
float. Then, if the price of the currency in the foreign
exchange market floats up or down too erratically or too
fast, the government's banker intervenes to buy or sell in
such a way as to moderate the change in price. Other
governments prefer to keep a firmer control of exchange
rates by revaluing, upwards or downwards, the currency
as often as they judge it wise. Whichever form of flexible
exchange rates is chosen, they remain important signals

about the strength or weakness of a nation's currency.

There is, indeed, no satisfactory substitute for this signal. When it indicates that total imports are rising in relation to exports, not just the government but all others whose business it is to keep a watchful eye on the nation's economy then see it as their task to examine the reasons and consider remedial action. For example, they might point to a difference in domestic costs between the two countries; and a comparative study may show a higher level of wage costs or a failure to invest in more modern plant and equipment. The signal provided by flexible exchange rates will compel an enquiry into why the disadvantage in the currency market has arisen, which in turn will lead to debate and discussion about the cause and a consequent change of policy.

But what happens when the two countries decide to have a common currency? The two governments then lose control of the exchange between the two currencies. No longer able to allow the Poorland currency to float or adjust the exchange rate, as other independent countries do, an important control over imports is lost. Richland becomes richer and Poorland poorer; and Poorland's government would be powerless to prevent the drain of wealth to Richland by the simplest and most effective of methods. It would also, of course, lose its power to impose the most efficient methods of exchange controls.

The supranationalists' rejoinder is that Poorland can receive regional aid and that this would be an adequate replacement. It works, does it not, in independent nation-states, so why should it not do so in the United States of Europe? There are several objections to it. In the first place, it takes time to decide whether it ought to be given. An area has to be blighted by a high degree of unemployment before steps are taken. People naturally have to lose their jobs and perhaps be out of work for an appreciable length of time before voices are raised and heard. Moreover, it is seldom that an area becomes suddenly depressed; the process tends to be slow at first and gradually gathers pace, so some people may go bankrupt or become unemployed long before regional aid is contemplated. Secondly, regional aid is by its nature arbitrary, for someone must decide the boundaries of the area to be assisted; a line has to be drawn, and the arbitrary line will include some who are not in need and exclude others who are, as no line can be drawn among tens or hundreds of thousands of people with such nicety as to ensure equity. Thirdly, regional aid, by requiring an increase in expenditure, calls for more taxation — a diversion of resources, theoretically from the rich to the poor. Whatever form of taxation is chosen, it must represent an added cost on a part of the economy that is capable of paying because it is successful in providing a sufficient number of customers with what they want. The tax, whether absorbed or passed on, will have the effect of eventually reducing the economic welfare of the public. By transferring this money by way of aid to another sector of the economy, it is buttressing something which for some reason has failed to satisfy the public. Regional aid may perhaps be seen as an act of kindness, as short term assistance to coax an area of the economy to do what the public would wish, but as long-term action it must serve to take away resources from where the consuming public had indicated in the market it would like them to be, and to direct them to where it has equally indicated it does not want them. The overall strength of the economy is thus lessened.

The next objection brings us to a recurring question about the exercise of power in a super-state: who are the beneficiaries? When regional aid in the form of money is allocated it has to be given to some people and not to others; and some get more than others. Submissions are

made for the funds available, representations and lobbying follow. Try as they might, it is a tall order to expect
politicians and civil servants to be so even-handed that
everyone in the assisted region gets a truly equitable
share. The task is beyond Solomon himself. In practice,
we can be sure that some will be more articulate and persuasive than others, and some will know how to get
rather more than their fair share and also know to whom
to make their overtures. The large companies will be able
to receive many millions of pounds to the hundreds for
the one-man businesses, but the very fact that one concern may succeed in receiving so much more money
makes it worthwhile spending a small fraction of the sum
in making the overture. The same fraction of what the
one-man business might receive may buy no more than a
packet of crisps. Thus the large company may be justified
in employing accountants, solicitors, PR men and pro-
fessional lobbyists to secure a share of the regional funds;
and the bigger the corporation the more it may justify the
expenditure. A regional policy cannot avoid being arbitrary in its effect; and what is arbitrary cannot avoid being
less fair than its architects would wish it to be. Finally, a
regional policy in a small country will be operated by the
government in closer proximity to the assisted regions
than would be the case in a super-state of over 300
million people. A greater understanding of and sensi-
tivity to the problems are then more likely. The further
away the decision-making, the more difficult the task of
doing what is most just and appropriate. A regional
policy directed and funded from Brussels can scarcely
serve the interests of all 300 million as well as each country deciding for itself how it should be done, but, it might
be added, in a truly small country there is no need for a
regional policy. Instead each country is itself a region;
and by being even-handed towards its whole population
with each part of the region-country treated alike, a

healthier (in both senses of the word) economy exists. Still, a common currency has an obvious attraction. Not only importers and exporters find life easier, but travellers of all kinds, not least the holidaymaker. How absurd that we should have to change our own money as we cross the frontiers. There was a time when a traveller could set off for the continent from London and cross one frontier after another with the same pocketful of coins; the gold had the same value wherever he went. Today's money, however, is intrinsically worthless; and therein lies a major difficulty with a common currency. If our money was all in gold or silver coins, minted to a universally agreed standard, a *de facto* common currency would come about tomorrow and each government would go on minting as much money as its supply of gold and silver permitted. If it had no gold or silver in the mint, no more money would be put into circulation. With bits of paper it is quite different. Some institution must be in control of its printing and decide how much of the currency is to be put into circulation at any one time; and quite plainly this institution cannot be the governments of the different countries. It can be just one country, and it might be said that the Deutschmark has *de facto* become almost the currency of the countries that fully belong to the European Monetary System. Were the Deutschemark to become *de jure* the common currency, all the other countries would simply leave it to Western Germany to decide currency policy. As neither France nor Britain would be likely to surrender so blatantly the control of an economy's pivot, we are left with only one possibility, a supranational authority. The Bank of England and the other central banks would then acquire a subordinate role.

Not for nothing is it called the Royal Mint. The sovereign's stamp is upon the coinage, and the sovereign's figure is printed on the paper money, because the sovereign alone for centuries has been the guarantor of our currency's value. Sovereigns in days gone by, when short of revenue might be tempted to manufacture money rather than increase taxation, with inflation the consequence. Modern governments do it often. This brings us to a problem that has blighted many government records in the post-war years — a failure to curb inflation. A common currency will entail a common rate of inflation, for a unit of a currency will be as valuable in one country as it will in another, just as the pound is the same in Norfolk as in Suffolk. Once the government concedes to the electorate that it is no longer responsible for the rate of inflation, it admits to a degree of powerlessness that pervades every function of government. It becomes a non-government. As Lord Keynes was reported to have said, "whoever controls the currency, controls the government." Of all the circles of interest that can be created artificially, perhaps none will cause more friction and disharmony than a common currency.

8

Pragmatic Europe:
Economic Commission For Europe

The origin of the Economic Commission for Europe goes back to 1947 when the United Nation's Economic and Social Council, by way of an experiment, set up a temporary organisation to "initiate and participate in measures for facilitating concerted action for the economic reconstruction of Europe, for raising the level of European economic activity and for maintaining and strengthening the economic relations of the European countries both among themselves and with other countries of the world". Such were its achievements in those post-war years that in 1951 the ECE was placed upon a permanent footing. The governments of thirty two countries of Europe have since become its members. They are: Albania, Austria, Belgium, Bulgaria, Byelorussia, Cyprus, Czechoslovakia, Denmark, Finland, France, East Germany, West Germany, Greece, Hungary, Iceland, Ireland, Italy, Luxembourg, Malta, The Netherlands, Norway, Poland, Portugal, Romania, Spain, Sweden, Switzerland, Turkey, Ukraine, USSR, the

United Kingdom and Yugoslavia. The United States and Canada also joined on the grounds that many of their economic and social problems were similar. Their participation in the work of the Commission is, however, limited.

For two reasons the ECE has attracted little publicity. As its purpose is to achieve co-operation between governments, it has only entered areas of activity when it first felt sure that national interests converged to a degree permitting consensus. No attempt has therefore been made to impose a decision upon an unwilling government or jeopardise the interests of a minority in a member country. Arguments between governments warrant a headline, for often they lead to something worse, a crisis in diplomatic relations, threats of retaliation and ultimately, as in times past, the march of troops. As such consequences fly in the face of all that the United Nations stands for, the alternative of seeking a consensus, quietly and patiently, is the only policy permissible for the ECE. However, it seldom excites news editors. The other reason is that, unlike the EC, it has never had to justify itself to taxpayers or lay claims to greater powers over others. While the Commission of the EC finds it necessary to spend millions of pounds upon public relations and is an ever-ready host to the media, the Economic Commission for Europe spends not a penny upon its promotion.

Nevertheless the work adopted by the ECE is intended to be conducive to consensus. Sixteen Principal Subsidiary Bodies have been set up; between them and the Commission there is a two-way flow of ideas about the programme of work to be undertaken. Its record over the years shows how diverse are the subjects covered by its committees; and although each of Europe's main industries are separately covered, it is notable that environmental issues are also included. The committees are semi-autonomous; they can submit to the Commission the matters they should look into, and while overall policy remains with the Commission, a free hand is given to the committees as to how they carry out their programme. Rules of order, procedural devices and protocol, each of which is so necessary when a conflict of interest may arise, are not laid down for the reason that such formalities are out of place. Nobody in the ECE treads upon another's toe because there is neither the inclination nor the power to do so.

The Commission itself meets in plenary session in the spring of every year for about two weeks. The previous year will be reviewed and the work programme agreed for the next twelve months. The occasion gives the opportunity to each of the committees to give an account of their activities and for it to be discussed and evaluated. Resolutions may be passed; and although a simple majority was agreed as being necessary, this rule has been dispensed with as the practice has grown up for the Commission to record a resolution as being passed only when there is a consensus. A proposer of a resolution does not press a vote; a division of opinion may be resolved by negotiations, and should these be successful the draft resolution is amended accordingly and resubmitted to the plenary session for approval. The representatives of the member governments are then able to go back to their capitals with a resolution carrying the weight of the Continental endorsement.

Is the work of the ECE thus made innocuous, so bland as to have no bite, making it no more than a forum for the exchange of information as to what the different governments are doing? If the latter were so, it would still be useful, although its record over the years shows it has achieved an important degree of international co-operation and, moreover, is capable of much more.

The following paragraphs set out some of the achievements of the ECE. Some of them are manifestly useful; others may seem less so, but if that is the case, it might be emphasised that every step taken by the ECE itself or its committees is the result of what individual governments have themselves wished. The ECE exists to serve the governments of sovereign states to enable them to work with each other. It is they who set the pace through their representatives attending the meetings of the ECE and committees.

The ECE's Inland Transport Committee, having been given overall guidance for the reconstruction of Europe's transport system after the chaos left by the Second World War, has since remained the only inter-governmental body concerned with the problems of trans-national transport for Europe. In nearly half a century of revolutionary change, in which many thousands of miles of new roads, a tenfold increase in motor vehicles, a revitalised railway system and a burgeoning of air traffic have enabled many tens of millions of journeys to be made every year across national frontiers, the Inland Transport Committee has done much to bring in the new era of popular travel and commercial traffic. At least fifty international agreements and conventions can be credited to the Inland Transport Committee.

Given that almost every country in Europe had in some way or another different laws or practices relating to transport, the task of bringing down these non-tariff barriers has been enormous, but success has come because governments have appreciated that these barriers inhibited commercial progress, quite apart from causing a curb upon individual freedom to travel abroad. The will of some thirty governments, however, is not enough: the mechanisms of co-operation had also to be put in place. The Convention on the Contract for the International Carriage of Goods by Road (CMR), in 1956, and the Convention on the Contract for the International Carriage of Passengers and Luggage by Road (CVR) in 1973, both of which were the work of the Inland Transport Committee, have been two of the necessary mechanisms for co-operation.

Among its other achievements, the Committee has devised a uniform system of road traffic rules and road signs, signals and markings, adopted throughout Europe, which may be a basis for a world-wide convention. To improve road safety and reduce air pollution and noise, the Committee has drafted regulations on the performance standards of motor vehicles and their equipment and parts. It has introduced simplified formalities at customs points for road transport by the guarantee system for the carriage of goods under customs seal in accordance with the TIR Convention. The major international road traffic routes, based on uniform design and construction, known as E roads, have been classified and numbered. The green cards system, well known to hundreds of thousands of motorists, that enable an insurance policy hitherto valid only in the country of origin to provide cover throughout Europe, was another product of the Committee. For the crews of commercial vehicles on trans-national journeys, inter-governmental agreements for insurance, driving permits and drivers' hours had been the outcome of the Committee's efforts; as have agreed international regulations for liability in the carriage of goods and passengers. The Committee has organised five-yearly censuses of traffic on the main international road routes and statistics of road accidents have thus been compiled. The Trans-European North-South Motorway (TEM) to link the Baltic states with South Eastern Europe and the Middle East has been inspired by the Committee.

In the area of rail transport the Committee has been responsible for the Customs Convention for the transport of passengers and goods by rail between the coun-

135

tries of Europe. It has acted as a medium for the exchange of information concerning many technical problems on the railways, which has led, for example, to the standardisation of automatic couplings. The European Agreement on Main International Railway Lines (AGC) was reached under its auspices. The Committee has made an important recommendation about where the marshalling yards for international rail transport should be placed. The complex and controversial subject of the health and quality inspection in the rail traffic of live animals, living plants and the food products of animals and plants has also been taken up successfully with a unanimous resolution passed to facilitate their international trade.

Comparable progress has been made also by the Inland Transport Committee to ease waterway transport between the countries of Europe. Nine achievements can be listed. The European Code for Inland Waterways (CEVNI) now exists which introduces rules of the road and signalling between vessels. On the waterways themselves a uniform signalling system has been brought in (SIGNI). Uniform standards have been laid down for waterways used internationally as well as for the vessels using them. The specifications of vessels have also been raised to a higher standard as a result of recommendations that have been agreed. More important have been a number of conventions approved by most countries in Europe about the liabilities that arise when vessels collide and the form of contracts for the carriage of goods and passengers. A study has been undertaken of the economic aspects of inter-connecting European river basins, including the economic implications of linking the Rhine/Main and Danube/Aegean Sea. There have also been studies of the most rational sites and the most efficient construction methods for port installations on inland waterways and the technical problems and their economic consequences for inland navigation. Another study has been done of the prospects for the development of inland water transport in Europe. The ninth achievement is the introduction of measures to promote the use of waterways for tourism. The Inland Transport Committee has also addressed itself to a number of other problems. There has been a study undertaken of the administrative, technical, economic and legal aspects of combined multi-modal transport with a view to making the most use of equipment and terminals. There has been a study, too, of the flow of traffic between East and West Europe. International instruments in the field of customs questions and other frontier formalities have also been introduced. The *Annual Bulletin of Transport Statistics for Europe* has been published. Seminars have taken place on the financial aspects on international transport infrastructure, on transport corridors and on the criteria for investment in transport infrastructure. The Committee has also been responsible for an international agreement setting out the requirements for the carriage of perishable foodstuffs.

According to the ECE's Report on its forty years' work *ECE 1947-1987,* from which most of the details in this chapter are drawn, the programme of the Committee on the Development of Trade was reconsidered in 1985. It was decided to redefine its activities as follows:
1. Analysis and review of recent and prospective trade trends, policies and problems;
2. Identification of all kinds of obstacles to the development of trade among ECE member countries, especially in East-West trade and endeavours to reduce or provisionally eliminate them, giving due attention to measures for the promotion of trade and diversification of its structure;
3. The development of market information, marketing

137

and financing techniques and improved business contacts;

4. Promotion of trade through industrial co-operatives;

5. International trade procedures, contract practices, trade aspects of regulatory and standardising activities and commercial arbitrations; and

6. Trade problems of the member countries of the ECE which are developing from the economic point of view.

Although these six areas may seem to lack any specific order of priority, they nonetheless indicate the extent to which the ECE is willing to further international co-operation in matters of trade and industry. Progress in these areas would afford inestimable gains in economic welfare for the people of Europe. If that progress has not been made, it is arguable that one reason is the pre-occupation of EC member states with the proposals for the single market. Again, it shows the importance of deciding the fundamental question of whether it is a "deeper" or a "wider" Europe that is desired.

Despite that difficulty, the Committee on the Development of Trade has made some useful advances. At each of its annual sessions, the Committee has assessed the external trade of member countries, especially looking at how the levels of trade and payments are decided, and how changes in economic structures affect the nature of international trade. *The Economic Survey of Europe* is published annually, containing a detailed survey of trends and analyses; it is a valuable and authentic guide for governments and business management. The secretariat of the ECE maintains an inventory of non-tariff barriers. Their number is immense and almost impossible to list completely, but governments have been willing to submit the specks in others' eyes without necessarily admitting the beams in their own. This inventory has become a useful instrument for the Committee on Trade Development in its deliberations, for non-tariff barriers will never be eliminated unless they are identified and recognised as such, as GATT itself has found. The Secretariat, as the only independent body concerned with international trade for the whole of Europe, is uniquely qualified to compile and disseminate another fund of knowledge — all the information about trading practices and policies and opportunities that is needed for the development of commerce. The Committee on Trade Development has also held a series of seminars on the promotion of trade attended by governments' representatives and business leaders. Of these a notable example was the Thessaloniki Symposium which examined the opportunities and prospects for greater international trade in Europe for the latter part of the 1980s; under the Committee's auspices has been the Group of Experts on International Contract Practices in Industry. Beginning with the engineering sector, the Group has been successful in introducing standard forms of contracts and conditions of sale for the export and import of products and services. The result has been fewer misunderstandings and less litigation between businesses in different countries, a matter of some importance when a conflict of law might otherwise arise as often used to be the case. Again, under the auspices of the Committee, the European Convention on International Commercial Arbitration was signed and ratified by twenty countries of Europe. This agreement was the outcome of several years work by the Working Party on Arbitration: it introduced means whereby an arbitrator may be appointed and questions of procedure may be settled, and it has also made available a set of arbitration rules which the parties may use if they wish.

The sheer weight of paperwork, much of it incomprehensible to the ordinary businessman and in a foreign language with which he might be ill-acquainted was once a major obstacle to trade across frontiers. Such was the case until recent years. In 1960 the Committee appointed a Group of Experts to examine these difficulties. The ECE Layout Key has been the product of their endeavour; this introduced the same layout for all exports and import documents, so that businessmen could understand at once the purpose of each document and its contents. Its success in Europe has led to its being adopted by most countries in the world.

Incomprehensible documents have given way to the mysteries of data processing and teletransmission as a deterrent to international trade, but the Committee's Working Party on Facilitation of International Trade Procedures, set up in 1971, has stepped in to rationalise the new practices and formalities and much progress has been made to prevent these details becoming obstacles to trade. In 1986 it introduced a set of rules to construe trade messages. Its efforts to remove legal difficulties about trade data, having been established in Europe, have evolved into the United Nations Trade Data Elements Directory.

Technical barriers have bedevilled the growth of transnational trade for many years and prompted in 1980 the GATT agreement on the Prevention of Technical Barriers to Trade. The latter has stimulated the ECE to consider what should be done in Europe. It had, however, ten years previously arranged a meeting for representatives of all member governments to attend and at some nine subsequent meetings, these barriers were reviewed, which led to the governments appreciating the dangers of their growth and the necessity to achieve some standardisation. There is now a series of *Recommendations on Standardisation Policies* and an ECE Standardisation List, which has enumerated various technical barriers likely to damage trade and also those amenable to government regulation.

The advance of technology, having given national governments the opportunity to increase the number of technical barriers to trade, has been recognised by the ECE in the setting up, in 1971, of the Senior Advisers' Group. These are representatives from the national governments, more fully known as the Governments' Experts on Scientific and Technological Co-operation. Rather than be a Committee that works out international agreements or drafts conventions for individual countries to adopt, the role of the Group has been more of a forum for the interchange of information that may lead to co-operation. Each year there is a seminar, and among the many questions that have been discussed are the environmental aspects of energy production and use, the importance of biotechnology for the future economic development, and the recycling of basic industrial materials.

The value of these discussions probably lies in the degree of unanimity reached. For these experts to be in broad agreement about what should be done is a powerful argument for some action to follow; they can return to their various countries to report on what has been said with a likelihood that their governments will be persuaded that a change of policy is desirable.

In addition, the *Manual on Licensing Procedure,* with which twenty-four countries are associated, is in the hands of the Senior Advisers, and is regularly brought up to date by them. They also maintain a register of bilateral agreements on scientific and technological co-operation. Not to be undervalued is the Group's opportunity to exchange ideas about government policy in the whole area of science and technology, and the consequent harmonisation that may ensue without friction or argument.

A comparable role is performed by the ECE's Senior Economic Advisers' Group. In 1984 they decided to begin work on what is called an Overall Economic Perspective for up to the year 2000, as a result of their success in preparing earlier such Perspectives. These have covered demographic and labour projections, variants for the main macro-economic indicators, structural changes, long-term investment policies, energy prospects and investment, evaluation of the factors determining scientific and technological progress on economic growth and an analysis of international trade flows and their projection.

Continued economic growth is now seen as having consequences for our environment that may have to be set against the gains to our standard of living. Yet it was the ECE that as long ago as 1956 began to study the connection. Since this book argues that the main case for international co-operation throughout Europe is the need to protect the Continent's environment, the potential role of the ECE in this major task ought not to be overlooked. Indeed, it is something of a tragedy that the member governments of the EC have allowed themselves to be diverted by Brussels from doing more in Geneva under the auspices of the ECE.

It was in 1956 that the subject of water pollution was studied, in particular how on the waterways it was caused by navigation, and this led to the setting up of the Committee on Water Pollution. The Working Party on Air Pollution Problems followed. Also, twenty years ago an ECE Meeting of Governmental Experts on Problems relating to the Environment was convened at the suggestion of Czechoslovakia; and Sweden proposed a similar meeting which evolved into the United Nations Conference on the Human Environment which took place in Stockholm in 1972.

An inevitable step for the ECE was then to introduce

for Europe's environment what was already in being for Europe's economy, namely regular meetings of Senior Advisers on Environmental Problems.

One of the first tasks of the Senior Advisers was to look at air pollution, and the outcome was the Convention on Long-range Transboundary Air Pollution. It was subsequently signed on behalf of thirty-five countries. With the Senior Economic Advisers, they held a joint seminar on the ecological impact of economic development; this was in 1975 and for once the seminar was justly so-called, since the ideas that were canvassed were indeed seminal, much of what has since been said and written on the subject having originated at the seminar. Not only then, but ever since, the Senior Advisers on the Environment have emphasised the need to take into account the effect on the environment that government decisions on planning and development may have. Governments now require no persuasion about this, and to help them put the proposition into practice, there is now the Group of Experts on Environmental Impact Assessment, appointed in 1982, whose purpose is to devise suitable methodologies to enable impact upon the environment to be assessed. The Group has also drafted bilateral and multilateral agreements for governments to adopt when they believe the environmental impact may cross frontiers.

Some countries in Europe have been more conscious than others of the importance of protecting its flora and fauna and their habitats. The Senior Advisers have therefore drawn up an inventory of the measures and legal instruments in the different countries with an evaluation of their effect. Governments can now draw upon the information for guidance on how to proceed, should they wish to take steps to safeguard their wildlife or improve the steps taken already.

More ambitious has been the decision of the Senior

143

Advisers to draw up what they call a Long-term Strategy for Environmental Protection and Rational Use of Natural Resources in ECE Member Countries for the period up to the year 2000, and beyond. To decide what were the trends and the objectives in each country was the first stage; and if perhaps the final conclusions of the Senior Advisers failed to make a headline in the tabloid press, at least governments throughout Europe can draw upon a body of information about what is happening in other countries to give them a clue as to what they might do themselves.

Economic growth, especially in the more populated parts of Western Europe, has given rise to a problem scarcely known to an earlier generation — waste. The Senior Advisers held a special conference on the Disposal, Treatment and Recycling of Solid Waste in 1975 and on Low and Non-Waste Technology in 1976. Both were occasions when ideas from one country could flow to another and the interchange was of great value to the large number of governments represented. Many of the ideas were scientific and highly technical, so a working party was subsequently appointed to study in detail the technology and compile the *Compendium on Low and Non-Waste Technology*. This is a continuing task as new ideas arise and it provides a data bank to which governments can turn for up-to-date information.

So long as a gentle breeze blows, the pollution of the air by one country may be a cause of at least annoyance and perhaps anger in another. Transboundary air pollution is thus a proper subject for the ECE as part of the United Nations. Seminars have been arranged, to which all countries were invited, to consider desulphurisation of fuels and combustion gases, the control of fine particles and pollution by the chemical industry. Each one led to the Senior Advisers being asked to make recommendations for countries to adopt. In 1975 the ECE

144

established a working party to decide how to identify and classify emissions of sulphur dioxide as a necessary first step to enable national governments to introduce abatement policies. The Convention on Long-range Transboundary Air Pollution, agreed in 1979, has been seen as an important move towards getting governments to curb air pollution. Nearly every country in Europe has agreed to it. The ECE is now in a position to monitor the progress made by each country in its efforts to reduce and eventually eliminate its pollution of the air. The work of the Senior Advisers has shown that it is not just sulphur dioxide that is a serious danger to our environment: other pollutants include nitrogen oxide and organic compounds which may add to the difficulty in detecting the cause of pollution. With the aid of the World Meteorological Organisation, the ECE is also monitoring the effect air pollution is having on the forests, the acidification of rivers and lakes and the effect of pollution on historic buildings.

As there can scarcely be economic growth without an increase in energy, the ECE has turned its attention to this subject in some detail; and in doing it has had the support of nearly every government in Europe. Since 1970, an *Annual Bulletin of General Energy Statistics for Europe* has been compiled and published by the ECE every year. Perhaps the central but by no means the only publication on energy that the Commission produces, it is relied upon by governments and other bodies as a valuable handbook in the making of decisions. It is supplemented by a long catalogue of reports and study papers on almost every aspect of energy policy in Europe. As with other subjects of policy-making, if individual governments have a source of authentic data about the trends and policies in other parts of Europe, the decisions they make, whether wise or otherwise, will at least have been made with knowledge of the essential facts.

Of all the many statistics that the ECE has published about Europe's energy, two are of special significance. Primary energy consumption has risen more than threefold in three decades; and from being a net exporter of energy, Europe now imports eleven per cent of its consumption. This being only a part of the price of economic growth, it is a part which may be difficult to afford at some time in the future.

The ECE has established separate committees for the coal, gas and electricity industries, all three of which have been transformed in Europe since the Second World War. That the changes have been considerably harmonised throughout the Continent is largely due to the interchange of information about trends, policies and technical data through the medium of these three committees.

The system of Senior Advisers has also been used in the case of energy. Brought together in 1979 for the first time, they may have been less ambitious than their colleagues in other areas, appointed before them. Still, numerous seminars on different aspects of energy have been convened, but perhaps of more importance for the future are the studies they have instigated on energy conservation and on new and renewable forms of energy. As with the other groups of Senior Advisers, they have overseen the gathering of a great mine of information upon which individual governments and other bodies, official and unofficial, can draw data of immense value in decision-making.

Perhaps the remaining areas of the ECE's work can be summarised in a few sentences. They include industry, agriculture, timber, water and "human settlements". If the immediate achievements seem less consequential than in the other areas, it would nonetheless be impossible to assess fairly the value of the information exchanged. For an individual government to grapple with a problem without knowing accurately what neighbouring countries are doing or have already done about it would be foolhardy. The ECE makes such foolhardiness unnecessary. These other committees might feel offended if all their concrete achievements were passed over, so perhaps just a few might suffice to show their value. The Committee on Housing, Building and Planning ("human settlements") has set up the International Council for Building Research,Studies and Documentation (CIB) which has had an enormous influence in raising standards throughout Europe. The Committee has also done much to harmonise building regulations in most of the countries.

Water, whether flowing down the rivers of Europe or washing the shores, heeds no national frontier. The ECE has been able to agree on various recommendations to protect coastal waters from pollution from land-based sources and these have been to a significant extent acted upon, as have other recommendations on, for example, water pollution from farm effluents.

That so little of these achievements is known to the public who are the beneficiaries is a comment upon two elements of the ECE's work. Harmony never makes news; and the ECE spends no money on public relations. In these two respects it seems to differ from that other Commission, of which our daily newspapers tell us something every day.

9

Churchill's Vision:
The Council Of Europe

There are some circles of interest that are large enough to encompass most of Europe: since 1949 when it was established, the Council of Europe has succeeded in identifying some of these circles and gone a long way towards furthering the interests within them.

It was Sir Winston Churchill in a broadcast in 1943 who first conceived the idea that, once the War was over, the peoples of Europe should organise themselves for the purpose of international co-operation. Five years later he saw it come about when 700 delegates from sixteen countries, with observers from ten others, gathered in The Hague at the Congress of Europe. They resolved that there should be a European Assembly of Parliamentarians, and that a charter should be drawn up and a Court of Human Rights set up.

Today, twenty-six countries, virtually all Europe except the Eastern bloc, send their representatives. Membership is open to any country in Europe, with the proviso that it recognises the rule of law and guarantees its people the enjoyment of human rights and fundamental freedoms; and the member country that fails to live up to these ideals can be expelled. Its declared objective is European unity: the term, though, is misleading, for there has been no attempt — and it is inconceivable that the Council of Europe would make the attempt — to merge the twenty-six countries into the literal meaning of a unity. Co-operation would be a more accurate word or a "coming together" to achieve a common purpose. The unity or "oneness" relates to the common interest, not to the countries themselves. The existence of the Council of Europe and the willingness of the twenty-six governments to support its endeavours indicate that there is a range of issues in member countries with a European dimension. The premise is that of this book: some things are best done by governments of nation-states, but there are others that are better done together with other governments that share the same interests. True, the Council of Europe has its flag and anthem; these have never been meant to supplant those of individual nation states, but to heighten the awareness of nearly 400 million people that they are Europeans too; besides the emblems serve as innocuous means to publicise the work of the Council to the majority of that number who are seldom conscious of what it achieves. In this respect it is, like the Economic Commission for Europe, in a public relations dilemma; harmonious agreement rarely gains a headline.

Both national governments and national parliaments are represented in Strasbourg, the seat of the Council of Europe. The Parliamentary Assembly of the Council can claim to be the first parliamentary institution of international status. It has, however, no pretensions to being a legislative body, nor can it "vote Supply". Instead, its role is deliberative and consultative.

The number of representatives from each country

150

depends upon its size; Liechtenstein, for example sending two and the largest countries, such as the UK, eighteen. There being no direct elections, the representatives are chosen from the national parliaments according to the strengths of the parties. The Assembly sits in party, not national, groups to emphasise that the representatives' first duty is to the people of Europe as a whole, and not their own nation-states. The Assembly usually meets in plenary session three times a year for about ten days. It may then debate any issue concerning Europe, the one subject excluded being defence, for this is the province of the North Atlantic Assembly, but this is of small importance as those countries that are in both the Council of Europe and NATO tend to have the same representatives going to both assemblies.

Members of the Assembly divide into thirteen specialist committees; these cover a broad range of subjects, the most important being economic affairs, education, culture, science and technology, regional planning, law reform, agriculture, health, social affairs and relations with the other European countries. The working languages in the committees, as in the Council generally, are English, French, German and Italian.

The Committee of Ministers is the Council's executive organ; it receives the recommendations made to it by the Parliamentary Assembly and decides on the action to be taken. The latter will be in one of two kinds; (i) a resolution which sets out the measures each member country should take to conform to a common policy of action; or (ii) a convention which becomes binding on the member countries once signed by them. The Committee of Ministers also receives reports from expert committees, members of which are drawn from member countries and these reports may also be the basis of either a resolution or convention.

There is no supranational quality about this procedure. The legislation springs from the elected parliamentarians or specialist experts in government service; it gains the *imprimatur* of ministers, but the legislation is made in the national parliaments. No decision can be made binding upon an individual country unless and until it is made so by its own legislators acting in accordance with its own constitutional procedure. Thus some countries may act on a resolution or ratify a convention, others may decline to do so or postpone their decision, for each resolution or convention marks out a circle of interest, leaving it to the elected governments and parliaments to make up their own minds whether or not their own national interest comes within the circle.

In addition to the Committee of Ministers, there are also conferences under the auspices of the Council of Europe, attended by ministers on specialist subjects. These have included justice, education, family affairs, regional training, environment, labour, culture, sport, local government and social security. These conferences will examine problems arising in these areas and if intergovernmental action seems desirable a report is made to the Committee of Ministers.

The Council of Europe has a Secretariat led by a Secretary-General with a staff of 800, and although doubts have been expressed about the need for so many, it is also a measure of the detailed work done by them in Strasbourg. Each of them is required on taking office to give an undertaking to disregard his or her national interests and any instructions from a government.

The Secretariat is divided into eight directorates. These are broadly the same as the eight groups of international activity undertaken by the Council of Europe. They are: (i) human rights and fundamental freedoms; (ii) social and economic affairs; (iii) education and culture; (iv) youth affairs; (v) public health; (vi) environment and natural resources; (vii) local government; and (viii) legal affairs.

Human Rights

The European Convention on Human Rights is perhaps the best known of the Council's achievements. Signed in 1950, it has now been ratified by twenty-two of the member countries. Any individual in any of the ratifying countries may submit to the European Commission on Human Rights a complaint that his or her human rights or fundamental freedoms have been infringed. If the Commission is satisfied that the complaint is admissible, it offers itself to the parties as a mediator for a "friendly settlement". Should this fail, the case can go to the European Court of Human Rights.

Member countries may also submit a complaint against another state. Greece, for example, submitted a case against the United Kingdom over events in Cyprus before the latter's independence; and at a later stage a group of countries, Denmark, Sweden, Norway and The Netherlands made a complaint against Greece for her infringement of human rights under the "Colonels' regime". The Court claims no supranational powers: it passes judgement but cannot, as it were, also pass sentence. This limitation has seemingly been of little consequence, for in practice its judgements have been looked upon as morally binding.

Social and Economic Affairs

A concerted social policy, its writ running across all Europe, would both secure a higher degree of social justice and lessen the effects of any particularly unfair form of competition where employers in one country are able to lower their wage costs compared with those in another country. Three conventions towards this end deserve more credit that they are usually given. The

153

EUROPE OF MANY CIRCLES

European Social Charter was signed in 1961, eighteen years before the EC's draft version was published. Fifteen member countries ratified it early on: Austria, Cyprus, Denmark, France, Federal Germany, Greece, Iceland, Ireland, Italy, Malta, The Netherlands, Norway, Spain, Sweden and the United Kingdom. Of those in the EC, Belgium, Luxembourg and Portugal have done so recently. The European Social Charter establishes the right to work in just conditions, the right of collective bargaining, the right to social security and medical aid, the right to vocational training, the right to protection of the family and the right to equal pay.

Each of the countries that have ratified the Social Charter is required to submit a bi-annual report on what has been or is being done to conform to the Charter. As these reports are open to inspection by other countries it can be seen whether or not the principles of the Charter are being carried out. Thus supervision falls short of any supranational element.

The Social Charter is supplemented by the European Code of Social Security. So far fifteen countries have agreed to it: Belgium, Denmark, France, Federal Germany, Greece, Ireland, Italy, Luxembourg, The Netherlands, Norway, Portugal, Sweden, Switzerland, Turkey and the United Kingdom. Its purpose is not so much harmonisation as to give a lead in enabling the people of Europe to receive security in sickness, old age, disablement and unemployment and to provide benefits for surviving spouses and those injured at work. Minimum standards are laid down and a supervisory system has been brought in on the lines of the Social Charter. Neither is imposed upon a member country, for ratification of the code and the consequent obligations remain a matter for each country to decide for itself.

There is also the European Convention on Social Security. Only seven countries have signed it; they are:

Austria, Belgium, Luxembourg, The Netherlands, Portugal, Spain and Turkey. The great increases in transfrontier trading, immigration and holidays abroad have given rise to the need to allow businessmen, immigrants and holidaymakers to take with them accrued rights to social security benefits. Although this is the reason for the Convention, it is clear that most countries do not believe it is in their interest to ratify it and, as with other conventions, no attempt is made to impose it upon them.

The Environment
Like the Economic Commission for Europe, the Council of Europe has been far ahead — some twenty five years, in fact — of the EC in raising environmental concerns and drawing attention to the effect economic growth has upon the environment. It was in 1962 that the Council of Europe voted a recommendation to the member governments to set up a committee to examine what should be done in nature conservation. The outcome has been a series of ministerial conferences on the environment, which have led to the European Conservation Year in 1970 and the European Architectural Heritage Year in 1975. Both heightened public awareness of these subjects and having made them a talking point have induced national governments, regional authorities and local councils to take many measures to protect both the natural and architectural heritage that would not otherwise have been taken, besides making owners, developers and others more conscious of their responsibilities.

Lacking powers of coercion, the Council has not been backward in exhortation. Publications have issued from Strasbourg to all the member countries on four matters of crucial concern to our environment: *Principles for the Control of Air Pollution* (1964), *Water Charter* (1968), *The Soil*

Charter (1972) and *The Ecological Charter for Mountain Ranges* (1976). They have served as an invaluable guide to officials in both national and local government when preparing proposals for policy; and they have also been weapons for environmental pressure groups to wield in debate.

That is certainly not all. The Council has quite a long catalogue of other environmental issues which it believes Europe must face. Among them are the protection of sites of ecological diversity, the control of freshwater pollution, the management of natural resources, the long term effects of land use and protecting the public enjoyment of the countryside. Detailed work has also been done on the protection of coastal areas, forests, soil conservation and on measures necessary to protect the wetlands and the threatened biotypes, such as the hedgerows in the Mediterranean maquis. In 1979 the Convention on the Conservation of European Wildlife and Natural Habitats was agreed, which became a major influence upon the Wildlife and Countryside Act, 1980. This Convention recognised that, as in so many environmental issues, national governments cannot succeed in isolation. The protection of migratory birds was seen as one of the first and most obvious examples of this.

The quality of our environment is to a large degree affected by the nature of the transport services. Yet a modern network of trunk roads which can so easily blight a landscape, is in the view of many a necessity if the peripheral regions are to share in the prosperity of the areas more favourable for growth. The Council of Europe has come down on the side of more trunk roads. This opinion has been shared by the Conferences of Local and Regional Authorities of Europe (CLRAE). Out of the seminars it has held have come the proposals to build Europolis (the linking-up of the cities that are hosts to the European institutions), and the link between Scandinavia and Central Europe.

Rural areas throughout Europe, even in the East, are witnesses to de-population. The European Conference on Regional Planning (CEMAT) has recognised the similarity of the problem throughout so many of the countries of Europe and has therefore sought remedies that might be applied generally. An interchange of ideas among countries is an obvious basis for detailed consideration and CEMAT has been the vehicle for this inter-change.

So much is but a modest summary of some of the areas of the Council's work. Its other committees have achieved a great deal. The potential capacity of the Council of Europe as a medium for inter-governmental co-operation seems limitless. That no attempt has been made to stretch it to anywhere near its potential is a disappointment to those who believe that in Europe there are many circles of interest. Those who believe the countries of Europe are capable of being treated as a single homogeneous entity will have no regrets; to them the Council of Europe should be shunted off onto the sidelines to make way for the supragovernmental machine. Sir Winston Churchill, who did so much to establish the Council of Europe, would, we may assume, be among the disappointed. After all, it was Churchill who declared at The Hague Congress in 1948 "We seek nothing less than the whole of Europe". He went on to add: "We welcome any country where the people own the government and not the government the people".

It is that ringing principle that has opened the Council of Europe to twenty-six countries. Not even its stoutest defenders would claim that such a principle decides who shall be admitted to the European Community.

10

Towards a Wider Europe

What are the steps forward to a wider Europe, and what practical form will it take? Let us, though, be clear in our minds what it must imply. In the first place, a wider European Community should be wide enough to open its doors to every country considering itself European. The desire to put a limit upon membership, which all advocates of a deeper Europe naturally will have, must be set against the disadvantage of excluding a country outside the Twelve from playing a part in a circle of interest to which it naturally belongs, thus weakening the power of the other countries in the circle to achieve fully the purpose of their co-operation. While an open Europe would militate against an integrated union of member states, it would strengthen the cohesion of each grouping of countries; indeed it would be indispensable for their effectiveness in working together. Secondly, a wider Community would recognise that, far from being some homogenous entity, Europe has such a diverse range of interests that unity would be neither necessary nor feasible. Instead, the different interests that groups of countries have in common need to be identified, and only when it is seen that those interests converge should an attempt be made to agree a common policy or a common programme of action. Thirdly, it is the people themselves, through their elected representatives, that are best qualified to assess the importance of their interests. The fewer the number of people that an elected parliamentarian represents, the less chance of a minority interest being overlooked. Bio-regional parliaments may, therefore, be the ultimate ideal, but in the meanwhile nothing larger than the existing national parliaments should decide whether new laws ought to be passed or new taxes imposed to enable a common policy to be put into effect. Fourthly, as many of Europe's problems have a dimension that stretches beyond the Continent and often around the world, a wider Community should strive to avoid damaging the interests of countries outside. Artificial trade barriers, the weapons of a trade war, raised by one state against another, have been shown by history to lead to bloodier forms of warfare, so as a general rule they should have no part in a common policy. If it is the case that an open world economy will enhance the prosperity of the human race. while doing less ecological injury than would occur if trade barriers were to persist, then a wider Community will be in a position to set an example, for there can be no open world economy without Europe.

Unfortunately, none of these four principles actuate the EC as it is now. On the other hand, there is no inconsistency between those principles and the way the Economic Commission for Europe pursues its objectives; almost the same could be said for the Council of Europe and EFTA. Would it be practical for, say, the United Kingdom to take a dramatic initiative, proposing that the Economic Commission for Europe should come to the centre of the stage and thereafter act as the catalytic agent for pan-European co-operation? Its credentials for the task are hardly to be doubted, and its structure, *modus operandi*, and, above all, its membership embracing all thirty-five countries are points in its favour. However, were the initiative to be taken by Britain a rupture with the EC might follow. As progress towards the single market would then be impeded, it would not be a course which many might wish to follow. The outcome could be a two-tier Europe, a little Europe of the Twelve and a wider Europe of thirty-five. The ideal would be an EC more ready to make it possible for such kindred countries as Norway, Sweden, Iceland, Austria and Switzerland to join, followed by others who have committed themselves to Western values by joining the Council of Europe, such as Turkey and Finland. Some of these countries have no taste for exchanging their own capital city for faraway Brussels as the centre for power, while others fear the potential wealth of a Greater Germany will enable her to dominate the Community in the future, no matter how many others may join. Such misgivings have prompted opinion, outside the Community as well as inside, to question whether it can ever in the future serve all the peoples of Europe.

However, if a reformed Community remains the ideal, it is undesirable to contemplate withdrawal by Britain. Yet a group of distinguished economists has written a paper to be published by the Centre for European Studies which concludes that were Britain to withdraw from the EC and rejoin EFTA, thus taking advantage of the European Economic Space, it would, in terms of trade, be to Britain's advantage.

As any proposal by Britain to reform the Community is likely to incur hostility from at least some of the other member states, the reasons given by these economists may have to be deployed. Firstly, they say the finances of

161

the Community remain precarious. Changes in the Common Agricultural Policy have brought only temporary relief from the threat of bankruptcy which arose as recently as 1987; expenditure may exceed existing revenue, but even if it is kept in balance, it will be due to the large and increasing contribution that Britain makes to the budget. Britain has been, ever since she joined, one of the two main paymasters of the Community. She has been not ungenerous to the other member countries over the last fifteen years, having paid over many thousands of millions of pounds.

The loss of Britain's money might be made good by Germany and perhaps France, but as most of the extra money would be spent on disposing of surplus foods of the kind for which neither Germany nor France are now primarily responsible, their taxpayers might not be too overpleased at having the additional burden transferred to them.

The next matter the economists' study draws attention to is the way the import-export ratio between the UK and the rest of the Community is steadily becoming worse as each year goes by. Before entering the Community, the UK tended to export more to the original Six than she imported from them. Once she joined, the position was reversed, the deficit amounting to over £10,000 million a year in manufactured goods with no sign of a downturn in the upward trend.

The two factors, both representing a cumulative transfer of wealth from the UK to the rest of the EC, may explain a trend which should be examined. It is the way the standard of living of the British people has declined compared with that of others in the EC. The United Nations agencies, in measuring a country's standard of living, take together three yardsticks: the number of cars, telephones and television sets owned *per capita*. Ecologically, this may be an unsatisfactory test for it is quantitive and not qualitative, and pays no heed to "the riches of the mind". Still, it provides a guide to what is happening, it is consistent with the principles by which the Community has sought to judge itself, and it shows the British people to be in a state of relative decline.

In a single market, prosperity is never uniformly spread, for there must be some areas where it is more advantageous to site production than in others. These are the growth points which attract investment, enterprise and labour with the consequent prosperity. As they get drawn to the growth points, so they leave the less favoured areas. When the United Kingdom, with the advent of an integrated canal and railway system, became a single market, the same process, though on a smaller scale, was seen. The Scots, Welsh and Irish, in their tens of thousands, were attracted to the growth points in England. There is no evidence so far that the growth points of the European single market will be on the periphery, but rather they will be in the golden triangle of Milan, Hamburg and Paris, with the south east of England a marginal beneficiary. That indeed has been the trend since the UK joined the Common Market.

If these trends persist, they will confirm the forebodings of the economists, and Britain may have to reconsider her relationship with the rest of the EC; so, too, may some of the other countries on the periphery, such as Portugal, Greece, Denmark and Ireland. Their position will be to a large extent dependent upon the future of the Common Agricultural Policy and the development of regional policies. So far these countries have benefited from one or both of them, but should they cease to do so, Britain will have allies in requiring another set of rules to govern the Community. The impact of the Common Agricultural Policy has also been raised by the economists. As the Treasury has estimated that the average family has had to spend about £16 per week more on

163

food as a result of the CAP than it would otherwise, a major transfer of purchasing power is evident. £16 per week more on food is £16 per week less on other things that the family would have preferred. Other industries have accordingly lost an enormous home market, and the cumulative effect of this annual loss must have led to a grave distortion in our economy. It may not be fanciful to assume that so many billions of pounds worth of lost sales must cause a fall in production that will account for at least a million jobs lost.

There is, however, an alternative way of looking at these higher food prices. Once we entered the EC, wage costs rose sharply and in many industries by 75 per cent. It is arguable that these made good the loss of purchasing power. This may be true, but wage costs in France, Western Germany and our other main competitors in the Common Market remained more or less stable in real terms. At once it put our exporters at a considerable disadvantage. As our industries, generally speaking, had paid comparatively low wages as the cost of living, especially for food, had been lower, there had been little need for them to increase productivity by introducing labour-saving plant and machinery. Our continental competitors had done just the opposite. Ravaged by the RAF, many of the Ruhr factories had to be rebuilt, while in France and Italy altogether new industries were being established. These countries had smaller workforces in modern factories; Britain had larger workforces in, more often than not, out of date factories, the worst of both worlds. Was this the main reason why our manufacturing capacity fell by no less than 20 per cent, with the consequent loss of employment? It seems to be so.

Lastly, Britain should not overlook the importance of North Sea oil to the Community's economy. So long as oil remains the lubricant and the power to turn the wheels in a modern economy, there is an advantage in having an assured and controllable domestic supply. This Britain can give; and about 40 per cent of Britain's oil has thus been given at a reasonable price, despite the wild fluctuations in the world market. It does not follow that these doubts must lead to Britain's withdrawal from the Community. Much will depend upon whether member countries make the changes which are necessary to create the single market. If it comes into being and with EFTA forms the European Economic Space, a transfer to EFTA could allow Britain to have the protection of floating exchange rates and the power of an independent regional policy to assist those areas whose prosperity had been lost to the growth points on the Continent.

However, these doubts do add up to an answer to those who decry Britain's ability to influence the Community. So long as Britain imports manufactured goods from the rest of the Community which are worth over £10,000 million more than their imports from Britain, any prospect of retaliation by the rest of the Community in matters of trade, so often predicted by the same people who decry Britain's role in Europe, is extremely unlikely, quite apart from being contrary to the rules of GATT.

To register the economists' doubts about the single market is important, for they reinforce, so far as Britain is concerned, the case for the Community to be primarily concerned with Europe's environment rather than her merchandise. Once the two concerns change places in the order of priorities, the argument for a wider membership becomes irrefutable. Then there is the influence of the United States. The agricultural trade war between the US and the EC has persisted from the time the Community began to sell wheat and dairy products to the Soviet Union at prices less than half those prevailing in the world market, reducing many an American farmer to

165

a state of penury, while others in their tens of thousands had to abandon their farms. It has done little to enthuse Americans with a desire to defend the member countries of the EC against the Soviet Union at a time when the threat in American eyes grows less as each month goes by. If the degree of freedom and the semblance of democracy in Eastern Europe matures into something that gains the approval of the US State Department, opinion on the other side of the Atlantic is likely to change. Kennedy's vision of the twin pillars will be eclipsed by the reality of Europe's division becoming so tenuous as to be of little consequence to the US. Innocent souls who believe the State Department and the CIA have played no part in increasing the membership of the Community from six to twelve might read Douglas Evans's *While Britain Slept;* its enlargement has been the core of US policy for Europe; and what she has shaped once, she can shape again.

Whoever pays the piper may have no desire to call for a different tune; and a reunified Germany has no reason to listen to any different music. The existing EC serves her well; her prosperity rises steadily, her share of Community trade goes ever upwards and should Economic and Monetary Union come, her supremacy will be complete. So it is unlikely that she will seek a wider Europe until the existing Twelve are fully integrated into a deep Europe. But paymasters have their rights; and the second largest has good reasons to call for a wider membership. The other countries might feel apprehensive; more members will make the slices of their cake smaller — that is, if the Common Agricultural Policy stays in its present form. Its reform has been canvassed for nearly as many years as it has existed; some changes have come, but it remains essentially the same. Yet how can we speak of the environment without discussing the countryside; and how can we look at the countryside without considering agriculture? As agriculture in the EC is governed by what is decreed under the Common Agricultural Policy, it follows that it is a powerful influence upon the environment. At the heart of the CAP is the system of guaranteed prices; as these are set at a level higher than what the consumer would willingly pay, they must have the effect of raising production to more than what would otherwise be the case. An artificially high level of output induced by artificial prices can be achieved by farmers if they force their land to yield the extra food. More land is then brought into cultivation, hedgerows and woodlands are ripped up, more nitrates and pesticides are applied. Both wildlife and the landscape itself are made the victims. Guaranteed prices are no friends to the rural environment. So this means that a Community that puts an emphasis upon enhancing the environment cannot allow the present system of supporting agriculture to endure. We cannot therefore be sure that the CAP will continue in its present form. The beneficiaries will be put in a dilemma.

The initiative, then, can come from Britain, the second best qualified to call for a change of tune. Before one of the twice-yearly meetings of the European Council, the views of the other governments can be sought; if at that stage or at the subsequent meeting of the political heads of state, the proposal is considered sympathetically, the door is then open for negotiations with the governments of all countries represented in the Council of Europe that wish to participate.

However, a less favourable reception is not improbable. Britain can then step towards Geneva and the Economic Commission for Europe. Is it too underfunded to pursue the role? For Britain to underwrite the cost would be a modest price to pay. Nor need the additional cost to the ECE be more than a bagatelle. There is already a substantial staff employed in the secretariat in Geneva.

167

The task of identifying circles of interest has been done frequently in the past and the business of arranging intergovernmental conferences has been theirs for decades. As the secretariat would be selecting circles of interest most likely to lead to successful co-operation, and none would be finally selected unless each government had indicated a willingness to take part, the prospect of agreement would be rather better than it is today on the eve of the European Council meetings. A failure to agree, in conditions so favourable to unanimity, would be a reason to despair of any common action for the benefit of the people of Europe. That, let us assume, is unthinkable. As nothing succeeds so successfully as success itself, a few agreements reached would have a persuasive effect upon those who wish European co-operation to prosper.

Let us look at how it might materialise. The destruction of the forests by aerial pollution is a concern of northern Europe; a programme of action agreed by all countries contributing to the problem is required; and the ECE is at hand to do the groundwork. The Secretariat would communicate with each government in turn, the UK having already signalled its support. Would they shrug their shoulders and say it was no business of theirs when it manifestly was so? A little diplomacy should ensure that one by one they would accept the invitation to the conference table. As with all such gatherings, preliminary work would have to be done before the conference assembled. Papers drafted by the secretariat and the individual governments about the scale of the problem, its future if present trends continued, the causes of it, and proposals for a common policy, including details of legislative changes and expenditure, and how it was paid for, would be obvious matters for consideration in the papers circulated. Once some areas of agreement were perceived, the conference could begin, with in due course a satisfactory outcome. It would, one hopes, have brought together Norway, Sweden, the Soviet Union, Poland, a united Germany, Denmark, Belgium, The Netherlands, Austria, Hungary, Czechoslovakia, Switzerland and France as well as the UK. The pre-conference work would have been unsatisfactorily done if more than one or two failed to attend or if a worthwhile programme were not accepted by all the countries most concerned. As to who presides or manages the agenda with the prime responsibility of ensuring success, it is an important detail that could be settled in pre-conference negotiations. After all, when it comes to the arrangements for an international conference, there are an immense number of precedents to follow in deciding any part of the *modus operandi*.

Any common policy or programme of action agreed at the conference would then go to the national parliaments to be ratified by the representatives of the people whose lives are intended to be benefited and whose money must pay for it. On past form national parliaments do not fail to ratify international agreements once it is clear that the benefit to the people outweighs the cost. Changes in the law and taxation can then be made to put the policy into effect, with the parliamentarians returning to the electors to justify what has been done in their name.

The destruction of the forests is but one of a long catalogue of European concerns that affect countries both inside and outside the Community. A successfully completed common policy on two or three of these would bring home the truth that Europe is more than the Twelve and that the Community must open its membership to many more or accept a lesser role in the work to be done. It is at this stage that Britain would be entitled to raise her voice by another decibel or two as a paymaster of what is so plainly working against her interest — the Common Agricultural Policy. Would it be appropriate for Britain to suggest that the Economic Commission for Europe might take a more lively interest in agriculture as the branch of Europe's economy with the greatest importance to the environment? To the logic of that our partners might turn a deaf ear, but the spirit of partnership might impel them to listen when Britain explained she felt no longer inclined to pay quite so much for their agriculture, while the balance of trade with them steadily grew more to Britain's disadvantage. It would then be Britain's degree of resolution which determined whether the CAP was brought to an end, with agricultural policy repatriated or reformed to protect the rural environment, rather than being an engine of destruction. Her withdrawal from a common policy for agriculture would, by definition, cause its demise; and were the Eleven to attempt to continue the existing policy unreformed, a search would have to be made for another paymaster.

The Common Agricultural Policy, having been the coping-stone of the edifice for so long, its dismantling, even if it is transformed into a common environmental policy, will concentrate the minds of the Commission in Brussels. Could they be eclipsed by their near-namesake in Geneva? The degree of apprehension might be decided by the extent Britain and other countries were determined that Europe should turn a shade of green. Initiatives rely on leadership; and a clear lead by one or more countries, either in or out of the Community, to act within one or more circles of environmental interest would be difficult for the others to ignore.

Assuming that by this time the ECE had been the instrument of some successful international agreements, not necessarily all in the field of the environment, the leaders of the Community would have to recognise the case for a wider Community in some form. The edifice of the deeper Europe, with its coping-stone shattered into twelve pieces or split into two, would be looking rather too fragile to beget much confidence. The time for new architecture would have come, and for a latter day Monnet to be heard.

The alternative scenario is that the European Council sees the necessity to invite countries outside the Community to take part in formulating policies that may concern them, with EFTA for example, to establish the European Economic Space. Desirable though this may be in some cases, each of the Twelve would be treated as part of a single mega-state; and this would both aggravate the democratic deficit (in the sense in which this book has redefined the term) and deny that circles of interest exist within the Community. A radical change in its constitution would therefore be required before the four conditions of a wider Europe were satisfied.

Whether it is the ECE or the EC itself that sets the pace, the evolution towards a wider Europe will see those outside the Community proceeding internationally; their national governments will be negotiating, their national parliaments making the changes in law and taxation, and ratifying the treaties. The member states, however, will be subject to the supranational powers of the Community's institutions. The strains upon the structure will soon become apparent, especially when one of the member states considers itself outside the circle of interest. Reverting to the example of a common policy being devised to save the forests of northern Europe, were the EC to take part in the negotiations, Greece, Italy, Spain and Portugal would find themselves embroiled in solving a problem not of their own making, and if subsequently called upon to give extra money to Brussels to pay for the policy, they might feel unjustly treated. Their feelings would give rise to a demand for something else in return (a common policy for Mediterranean pollution, perhaps, for which northern Europe would pay) or at

171

least there would be some friction that ill serves a partnership. The very supranationality of the EC seems therefore to have within it the seeds of self-destruction. Once member states saw the merits of each of them being able to opt in or out of a common policy in a reconstituted Community, a major step would be taken towards adopting the other principles of a wider Europe. The brakes would be off and all countries, wherever they may be in Europe, would see the means of making progress as far and as fast as they individually felt it desirable. Those already members of the Council of Europe, having experience of successfully working together, would be the first to see what could be potentially achieved. This would bring new life into its Parliamentary Assembly in Strasbourg, and with it a realisation that the role of the European Parliament was correspondingly less. In a Europe of many circles, a supranational parliament can ultimately have no place; in the short term it debates and reports upon agreements that are or may be reached, but only in so far as their own constituents in the Twelve are affected; in the longer term, their role declines as that of the national parliaments comes to the fore. Eventually it fades away, the Parliamentary Assembly of the Council of Europe becoming the consultative body of parliamentarians that can be an initiator of ideas and a sounding board for opinion.

The future of the European Court of Justice will depend upon the extent to which the single market is achieved. If all member-states accept the three hundred changes to bring down the most damaging non-tariff barriers and conscientiously enforce the regulations and directives aimed at removing them, there may be little for the Court to do in the future. As with the European Parliament, its work will diminish as other methods of international endeavour are seen to bear more fruit. The Twelve must still find a use for it, but it is hardly within

172

the bounds of probability that the other twenty-three countries will wish to submit to its jurisdiction if the laws made to carry out a common policy are made by the national parliaments. These laws, being domestically made, require to be interpreted and enforced domestically. Only when community law is touched upon can anyone, whether an individual, corporate body, government or the Commission of the EC, petition the European Court of Justice. Of course, some Community law may still be made, but as the wider Europe evolves, its importance will fade until the European Court of Justice may have only occasional work to do. The common policies would still be enforceable. As each one was ratified by the national parliaments by legislation, the jurisdiction of the national courts of justice would be extended automatically, just as it is when any other statute or ordinance is passed. Anyone aggrieved by the new law not being complied with would therefore have rights of redress, and that would include citizens of another country, as it does now.

Does the Commission also fade away? It could have a more useful function than ever before. If the scenario outlined earlier in this chapter were to materialise, there would be an element of competition between the Commission and the ECE. The introduction of the European Economic Space would enable the Commission in Brussels to have a secretarial role with the members of EFTA on economic matters which might spill over into other fields. The EES, however, would represent a very large circle, and probably too large for other than a very few common decisions relating to trans-boundary trade. Would the Commission then recognise that there were lesser circles to be served? The answer would decide the Commission's place in a wider Europe. An insistence that the Commission remains a supranational executive with the authority of the Treaty of Rome and the Single

173

European Act will retain the hope of a deeper Europe of the Twelve, but afford no prospect of influence prevailing over thirty-five.

But is there any need to speculate on whether the Commission or the other institutions would change? Neither nebulous dreams nor detailed blueprints matter much beside what is certain about Europe today. Throughout all its thirty-five (or more) countries, there is a sense of interdependence that has never been felt before. The reasons are several. Frontiers are crossed by both people and goods on a scale unthinkable a few decades ago, so for many millions of Europeans they no longer mark out the bounds of human and commercial relationships. The frontier post, having become a minor irritation for so many, is seen as an irrelevance by the great legion of Europeans who feel sure that the Continent's environment is in peril. But the darkest of all the clouds across Europe seems now to be passing over, and, beyond, some rays of light are seen. What is happening in Prague, Budapest, Warsaw and in Moscow itself makes good news politically. However, it is what a handful of technicians did at Chernobyl that makes us realise how environmentally interdependent we are, from the Atlantic to the Urals.

This sense of interdependence cannot go away now. It makes about five hundred million people believe they are of Europe. To infer that they must also be governed by the same laws and treated as if no differences existed between them is false logic. Whether or not the leaders of the European Community perceive that distinction will decide its role in the wider Europe that is now inevitable.

11

A Last Word:
Europe On A Human Scale

"Politics" said Lenin, "answers the question: who does what to whom". As one of the few political philosophers who was also a practitioner — and none more successful in the art than he — the dictum is not to be ignored. Politics then is about power, and power over people. Whenever a shift of political power is mooted, it might thus be wise for those over whom the power is exercised to ask some questions as to what the outcome will be. In particular, we might be wise to ask whether the shift will have the effect of concentrating power over our lives into fewer hands or whether power will come closer to ourselves. To call to mind an example of a politician or official proposing that power should move from himself at the top of the pyramid down to those below is extraordinarily difficult.

Democracy, as this book has defined it, is the diffusion of power. When power is spread down to every individual so that each has a more or less equal share, democracy is as perfect as it can be. Perhaps that makes

Robinson Crusoe the only man to have enjoyed democracy in its sublimest form. Such a diffusion of power could still, with a little forbearance, be achieved with a dozen shipwrecked sailors on their island. A modern society, in rejecting the principles of *laissez-faire,* has to acknowledge a necessary shift of power away from the individual to some centralised authority. But it puts democrats in something of a dilemma. In a very small state — Liechtenstein, let us say — there can be a considerable degree of interventionism or state control without the individual citizen being left with a feeling of powerlessness, that he cannot knock on the door of the Prince and ask him to put matters right. The larger the state, it must follow, the more this feeling of powerlessness grows. Perhaps the ultimate feeling of powerlessness arises in the United States where millions believe that the power of a single vote is so insignificant that only a minority troubles to vote for a President.

We must also ask ourselves a second question: who is seeking this shift of power? The voice may come from a puppet on a string, a minor politician or a hack columnist, paid and courted by others as well as his editor. At the time of the referendum in 1975 on whether we should remain within the EEC, a list of these hirelings was compiled and on it, sad to relate, were some well-known names. The paymasters, directly or indirectly, were some of our equally well-known business concerns.

Then there is the question: why is this shift of power sought? Money and power are the two spurs that move most of us. The pursuit of money is usually patent enough, with visible signs of money made and money spent. Such ambitions can be checked by law and taxation, and the danger to the rest of us minimised; and these ambitions may not be misdirected when the entrepreneur is the mainspring of wealth creation. On the other hand, the pursuit of power over others is never patent, and seldom are there visible signs to prove it. More likely is it to be cloaked in fine words, a plea for a good cause or the quest for idealism. And it is all the more dangerous when urged with sincerity as it may well be. Presidents and Prime Ministers are naturally sincere in thinking they are somewhat better at exercising power than others. Such national leaders are seldom lacking in self-esteem, nor loath to seek a little more of it. There can indeed be a correlation between the gathering of power and the growth of self-esteem. The enjoyment of power is evident enough to anyone who comes near to people who wield it. Equally, to be with those forced to relinquish power is to witness feelings of hurt, anger and despair. How right Lord Acton was — power does most certainly have a corrupting effect.

Sincerity or good faith is not the point. As John Stuart Mill put it, "good government is no substitute for self-government". No matter how benign the man possessed of power over our lives, the principles of democracy are contradicted. The concentration of power is inherently against the interests of those over whom it is exercised. The loss of freedom to the latter may be a necessary price to pay in order to live in a modern society; political or civic power must shift to a central point in any community above the smallest size, but when it comes to the kind of power great business corporations can wield over the public, we have to ask again that third question — why? A business capable of satisfying the public does not need protectionism, which means protection by the state against the desires of the public. It thrives on the freedom of the market place. Only the business that fails to satisfy the public goes to the state to ask for intervention, which is an accretion of power to the state against the public. The honeyed words of special pleading soothe the ear of the public as a lobby persuades the state to take this power, and they should be on their guard.

In a small state, not Liechtenstein's size, but in, say, Norway or New Zealand, this special pleading can be answered by a vigilant public, for the very size of the state enables a few small voices to be heard loudly enough.

What, we may ask ourselves, would happen in a United States of Europe, with power over the economy concentrated in Brussels? Democracy is difficult enough in any large state, and many argue it cannot prosper, at least not as it should, in any nation-state with a population exceeding twelve millions. Fortunately most countries in the world are no more in size, so the long-term prospects for democracy in the rest of the world are favourable. In none of those countries do we hear of any burning desire to surrender their independence and merge with neighbours to form a super-state or federal union. Perhaps most of them, having won their freedom and independence in recent years, appreciate them rather more than the countries of Western Europe, which ironically were once their colonial masters.

A diffusion of power is compatible with a European Community. But, and it is a very large but, the Community itself must be on a human scale. There can be no human scale when power shifts so far away from ordinary people that no direct link can exist between them and those who wield power over them; and the link must be short enough to convey feelings of closeness in both of them. It is just as important for Herr Grossman, the powerful man in Brussels, to feel close to Sean O'Kelly over in Connemara as it is *vice versa*. In one case, a sense of responsibility is evoked, in the other a belief that an injustice will not be overlooked. But is it really feasible for over 300 millions of Sean O'Kelly's fellow citizens to have anything other than feelings of powerlessness? True, a federal union permits the member countries to retain some powers; and the Minister of Transport may

178

decide whether a by-pass will be built for one town or another, but the total amount of money available for him to spend will have to be allocated by a supranational authority; and the Minister of Education may introduce some legislation as to what should be taught in primary schools, but the major decisions about higher education leading to qualifications will have to be harmonised and settled federally.

As to the idea that democracy can be served by some European Parliament, that some 400, 500 or 600 men and women, sitting in some central city such as Brussels or Strasbourg, can represent over 300 million people, no-one can seriously argue that any meaningful link would exist with either Sean O'Kelly or any but a very few of his fellow citizens on the Continent. How many of his constituents can an MP in Westminster meet in a year to have a conversation of any consequence? If a thousand, that is twenty on average every weekend throughout the year, and no MP can do that. Yet that's not two per cent of his electorate. Given a constituency seven times as large, the lady or gentleman in Strasbourg would be working hard to have a sustained conversation with one out of a hundred of the constituents in the lifetime of a Parliament. And who would the one per cent be? Not John Smith who turns a lathe in one of the thousand factories in the constituency, nor Tom Brown who drives one of the thousand buses, nor Mary Jones who teaches in one of the hundred primary schools. The one per cent may include the managing director of John Smith's factory or the manager of Tom Brown's bus company or the chairman of the governors of Mary Jones's school. Access to the MP with 750,000 electors will be difficult, and we can be sure of the kind of people who will succeed in treading a path to him at those week-ends when he journeys back to the constituency. It is the same in the United States. The senator home from Washington is a remote figure.

No true link is forged between Senator and ordinary citizen; and no Senator would pretend it was. In a federal union of 300 million people, parliamentary democracy on a human scale is simply not a practical possibility.

Only a Member of Parliament with a high degree of arrogance would deny the value of a conversation with John Smith, the machinist or Mary Jones, the teacher. A recent television programme or an article in the tabloid press may have influenced their view unduly, and may echo what was heard in the canteen or in the bar of the King's Head, but the intellectual quality of their view is not the point. The MP may be much disheartened to learn that John Smith knows nothing of the big debate in the House last week, and he may even despair at Mary Jones seeming to be interested only in the importance of another zebra crossing to her school. If such issues are important to John Smith and Mary Jones then it is important that democracy puts them on the agenda. Democracy self-evidently fails when it fails to do so. Over twenty-five years of being a Member of Parliament have taught the author how crucial it is to have these sorts of talks with constituents; they bring one face to face with the realities of life as ordinary people see them; they bring one down to earth, which is good for the character; and, above all, they give one an insight into the hopes and fears of the great majority.

Parliamentary democracy on a human scale, however, is more than a matter of being in touch with, and sensitive to, the views of ordinary people. It is a two-way process. The essence of parliamentary democracy, it may be said, is that the laws the people must obey and the taxes they must pay are decided by their representatives, and, because they are representatives, they must make themselves accountable to the people. A general election once in four or five years is a part, but probably the weakest part of the way in which Members of Parliament make themselves accountable. Modern electioneering has changed the relationship between MP and elector: gone are the great meetings in the Town Hall when the candidate, facing an audience of hundreds, was forcefully questioned by his opponents and a thousand votes could be lost by his answer; gone, too, are the verbatim reports of all his speeches in the local newspaper; and instead we have the television screen focused on the national leaders while individual candidates spend most of their time hurriedly canvassing from door to door. It has made our existing MPs with 60,000 or 70,000 constituents, willy-nilly, less accountable in any general election.

But what may we expect in a Euro-constituency with seven or eight times the number of constituents? Whether during or between elections, the danger will be the same. The Euro-MP will be accountable to a small minority only; and human nature — or the instinct for self-preservation — will decree that he had better make himself accountable to those who have the most influence among the 500,000 or more he is trying to represent. An executive council of some kind, consisting of probably no more than a hundred people in his own party, will have chosen him as their standard-bearer, as "our candidate", and they may speak of him with some proprietorial feeling. They themselves will have been elected by the party's branches in the Euro-constituency, and will thus come from the whole area of numerous towns and many villages or an entire conurbation. To make himself accountable to them alone will keep him busy enough on those week-end visits back from Brussels and Strasbourg. What price, then, that independence of judgment that Edmund Burke spoke about with such eloquence to the electors of Bristol? No doubt, he will try to make himself accountable to others. Again it can be only to a statistically insignificant number of people, but

181

in terms of local power and influence they will inevitably be the most significant. Accountability, as a principle of parliamentary democracy, must itself be on a human scale. The size of a constituency is crucial to its practicality; and no matter how hard the Euro-MP tried, his accountability to 500,000 constituents could only be a sham and a charade.

No, Europe on a human scale must be something radically different from the dream of the supranationalists. The Community must embrace all of Europe, for environmental and human needs cannot be met on a lesser scale. It must be an open Europe, for a Europe that is commercially isolationist in pursuit of the goal of self-sufficiency is manifestly not fulfilling the economic human needs that are better satisfied in the markets of the world. And it must be a democratic Europe. Small, or comparatively small, nation-states should decide for themselves what is most appropriate for themselves; and when they decide for themselves that their interests converge with one or more neighbouring nation-states, then a circle of interest can be formed and within that circle they can act together for the common advantage of the people who live in the circle.

Europe has many overlapping circles. That we are failing to employ the means to identify them and the mechanisms to act within them is a sad commentary on how far the idea of European co-operation has moved away from serving the interests of ordinary people.